Hildegard Khelfa

EROTIC
SHORT STORIES

© 2010 Hildegard Khelfa, 2010, Neuburg Donau
Production and Publishing House: Books on Demand GmbH, Norderstedt

All rights reserved.
Any form of use needs permission of the authoress and the publisher.

ISBN: 9783842328570

For the two lovers and for all who love life.

Contents

Foreword

It was on one of my walks along my beloved river, when I visited that hidden place of my childhood. The morning mood was clear, still a bit foggy, but the first sun shine was clearing the dust on the water surface. Cormorants flew disturbed from my presence, about twenty swans where gliding majestic on the surface. The sky changed from golden pink clouds of the awaking day into a gray blue heaven, five wild goose where on their way to a very near breading place. It was great and I really loved to be there so much.

I was just listening to the soft murmur of the water, the twitter of the wood birds, watching my dog who was jumping into the water and just trying to catch a wood stick, when I heard her warm laughing. A woman came nearer. I had never met her before. She had wood honey brown hair, blue and clear eyes, her smile was open and friendly and she was walking straight and with self confident steps. "I saw you and your dog and was nosy what you are doing this early time of the day!" She introduced herself as Hanna, from "Johanna". We started a friendly talk and soon where laughing and sharing thoughts and little anecdotes – like old friends. Sometimes you meet people and feel a very special connection. Thus was the beginning of a very inspiring friendship which lasted the winter and one spring – and on a virtual way is still continuing.

We met again, occasionally as well as planned. Our conversations touched every part of life, but circled often around living life as intense as possible. Quiet interesting, especially because we agreed in so many points.

Once I saw Hanna only from far away, but that time she was not alone. I was on my way to my hiding place, but stopped when I watched her leaning against a tall man, who's back was turned into my direction. So I got no details, just caught a glimpse on his muscular body. They did not even hear me and I was able to stop my dog in time, so we just took another direction, but I found myself smiling. About two weeks passed, I was looking out for her – but no life sign. Then one morning, I was just walking my favorite way, when I heard Hanna calling my name. And there she was.

"I have something for you!" Hanna told me a bit breathless and gave me a bag, filled with a little notice book, cards, printed pages and some photos. "What is this about?" I asked her. "You told me, you are writing books. I have something for you, it is very personal but I thought you may like it or integrate it into a novel or something else." "Well, I will read it of course, but why don't you try a book by yourself?" "I do not want it to be published under my name and to be honest, I cannot really write very good, I am more a drawer and love to do fiber crafts. Also, I thought, I want to give this to you as a thank you for our intense conversations. Maybe you draw some pleasures or inspiration out of it." I was really touched. "But that sounds like a fare well for me." "Yes, I will move away soon, it is time for a change in my life." She was smiling again. "Has this something to do with that man?" I smiled back. "His name is William, where did you see us?" I told her and found her with a huge grin. "Oh, well, I remember that day. Read it, you will understand it all. I only have one wish, that you publish it in English." "Hanna, I am no native English speaker, I can speak that language, but my mother tongue is

German and I cannot afford any translator. It would be no perfect book and the readers may be annoyed to find a number of grammatical cruelties or a whole book which seem to be a strange form of German-English." "Please try your best, I am just scared that some people may recognize me, when you publish it in German." "But I could easily change your names, Hanna, I could use any forename, you would prefer instead. You can choose them, if you like." "Yes, I know, but I want that to be the story of us and besides, it would be nice to read a book with our names. Just a little vanity, I think. Please do it for me, for our friendship." "Well, let me read it first, I do not want to give any empty promises, I do not know yet, what you wrote, okay?" "Okay, that seem to be fair to me. Now, I have to go. Take care, Hilde." "Take care, Hanna." We hugged and she walked back, leaving me with a smile and a little regret.

Anyway, I was so nosy that I hurried back home. I had no other appointments that day, so there was plenty of time to start reading her diary and notices. Soon, I forgot the world around me and could not stop reading. Never before, I had found so open and free erotic lines. And I now understood her wish to publish it in English and not in our mother tongue, not to mention our home town.

That is, how I started to sort the stories over the next days and weeks, following in the first part those entries from her diary, while I had to include the letters and notices from the printed pages. I hope that both of them will be content with my interpretations.

And I hope, my dear reader, that you forgive me my imperfect English.

I will now try my best to tell you about the stories I found under all those papers, the stories about Hanna and William.

Chapter 1: Bent Over With Black Laces

Step for step she heard him coming up the stairs. Her body was shivering from excitement while she bent over the little black leather chair, already waiting for him, black laces all over her body. He turned the key. She heard him waiting, maybe confused a little not to receive the usual and expected longing kiss. She found herself smiling. He closed the door careful and silent, sensing his surrounding like a panther, listening. She felt the sweet wetness between her legs, imagining the tension of his muscles and the very special way of his moves. Steps. He came nearer, smiling now because he sensed her flagrance. "Hypnotic" from Dior, that little red bottle of sweet sins... He saw the shine of candle lights through the glass of the bedroom door and left his baggage right on the floor. She heard him undress the jacket. It was hard to stay there, bent over that chair, the butt direction door, while all her impulses and longing wanted her to jump into his arms, but she knew it would be worth. She heard him undress and felt shivers of lust through her

body when she heard his manly voice: "Soon, honey..."
He knew. He always knew her desires. Her hips started
to move, as her body started to react on his presence.
She knew he was nude - now. Silent steps of his bare
feet on the ground and slowly the door was opened.
"Wow" he said and jumped behind her like a tiger,
holding her hips in his grip. "You little devil, but I like it,
bad girl you". Hmm, the touches. She was silently
giggling, pressing her hips towards him, wiggling her butt
and turning a bit her head, to receive his longing tongue,
exploring his mouth the way he did with her. His hands
seemed to be everywhere on her body, knowing her
favorite places with the experience of a lover who love to
give pleasures to a woman. She felt his hand touching
her clit, while the other hand started to circle around her
vulva, sharing the sweet wetness with the whole area of
lust. But she was in need, she knew she would get more
later, now she just wanted to feel him. "Take me wild"
she murmured, her face deeper than usual. "I need you
now" and she moaned with lust when his erected
manhood glided slowly, so slowly into her pussy. He
played with her. "Take me wild now, please" she begged
again, pressing her hips hard again him, describing little

longing circles. He left his fingers around her clit, touching her the way she loved it, always taking care to use her wetness for more pleasure. Then he gripped her hard and tender the same way and started to take her as wild as she needed it sometimes. Her lust and moaning fired his desire and she was so ready for him. How much he wanted just to explode, to let his sperm go into her cave of lust but he breathed and gave things little more time, rubbing her clit now a bit harder, while she felt already the waves of the coming orgasm. He knew that she needed to be hold harder now, trying to escape and longing the same time. She loved that game and so he caught her, was holding her and showed her his strength. "You stay here, baby, you are mine now" while he pushed faster now, she felt already the tension inside her body, her legs started to shiver and her back bowed. "No" she whispered, trying to free from his grip, trying to repeat the little catch, the little play of strength but of course he was too strong for her and while he hold her back with one arm and continued playing with her clit and taking her with his penis, she couldn't hold it anymore. The orgasm came with all its power and she screamed from it. "Let me see how you come" she begged, so he turned her round and ejaculated all over her breasts. They hugged and where holding each other a little while, not even aware of the fact that they where laying on the cold floor. "God" she said, "That was awesome!" and felt her muscles getting weak. "Come baby, lay down there". He pushed her careful and tender on their airbed where he opened her legs and started to lick her juices, holding her with his strong arms until he felt her tension, saw the changes of her vulva, the little erected nosy clit and heard her desire growing, until she came directly under his mouth and tongue. Sweetness all around her. He loved to drink her juices and she loved to feel that. "Welcome home" she said. "Hello baby, I was missing you".

Chapter 2: A Very Special Appetizer

They were sitting down in the new opened restaurant. For that special occasion the decoration was made very weird: long covers on the tables, strange nets or shawls between the groups of seats, here and there middle age century's looking light. The waiters wore old monks' robes and the only light on the table was a very strange combination of candle on the tables and fake fireplaces with a little red electrical glow in some of the corners. The half darkness had something unreal but also the advantage of a very special private sphere. While being led to their place, she watched a young couple kissing, feeling obviously unwatched. She smiled.

"What is in your mind, baby?" he watched her curious. She made her most innocent view. "Nothing, love, just hungry". They opened the books the monks had brought. Strange names of food, strange names of drinks. Interesting! They chose and wanted to start a conversation, when one of the monks obviously was stumbling over one of those shawl-decoration and let two glasses and his metallic tablet fall with a big bang. A moment, she could perfectly use. While her mate still observed parts of the scene – too much was hidden, she was able to glide under the table cloth. She opened his legs. "What are you doing, honey?" he laughed but that moment, one of the monks came to bring the drinks. "Did you chose the menu?" he asked. "Yes" he answered and started to point on the chosen numbers and ordered for both of them. A moment she used to open his zipper and free his erected penis. He wanted the monk to go, but he tried to make a perfect job. "Is your accompany coming back soon? We can offer a little appetizer first, our guests get some free specialties this week to celebrate the new opening. Maybe you prefer the cold plate for two?" she had slowly opened her mouth, wetting her lips and brought them over the head of his penis, drawing little circles with her tongue. He breathed and tried to stay unimpressed in front of the waiter. "Yes, that would be great, thank you very much. We take the plate for two." The waiter meant it good. "We can also advice a little extra liqueur for the lady. It is free too, you can chose but the ladies love especially our little cream of the house liqueur". She brought his penis deep into her mouth now, licking and sucking it, enjoying his soft skin and the erection. "Yes, thank you" His voice was changing a bit and he breathed harder. "Excuse me Sir, are you okay?" The waiter was concerned. "Yes, everything at its best. Can you please bring the drinks, I am very thirsty today." "Yes, of course, Sir". She was gliding with her tongue around her mates shaft, up and down, holding her hand around him, touching his balls careful with her other hand. She was doing it faster now, longing to let him come. Being aroused herself, she sucked and licked, played with him, full of desire to feel him gliding into her as well. "You will pay for that, honey" he said, "Wait what I will do with you today". She swallowed her giggling and continued until his hands came down to press her head into the rhythm he needed now. She followed. "Yes, baby, oh yes". His voice was rough now. He leaned back and closed his eyes. "Go on, baby, oh God, I love you". She followed the rhythm and tried to stay silent because the desire brought waves of lust through her own body. "So, Sir, the drinks. The plate will follow soon." "Hmm" her mate responded, "thank you" with a very rough voice. "Are you sure, you feel good? You have sweat on your face, do you need a doctor?" "No" he answered, "Leave me alone please." The waiter left, torn between feeling offended and concerned, looking direction bathroom for the lady who was with his guest. That moment that very same lady felt the explosion of sperms and she swallowed his tasting spices, allowing him slowly to leave her warm mouth, kissing his penis and his balls and carefully glided back to her place. Her face pure pleased innocent looking devilishness. "So, that is the plate for two?" she asked him. Well, I had my very special appetizer already, but we can go on to enjoy this together." She grinned broadly. "Are you okay, love, or do you need a doctor?" Her giggling vanished back to innocence, when the waiter came with another little drink for her. "I am glad you are back, I think your friend was not doing fine" he whispered. "Oh, don't worry, he is very fine now" she answered and took her glass for the little toast of love.

Chapter 3: Blind Date With a Soldier

She was cleaning her teeth in the bathroom, smiling happily about the calm and pleasant day. He was a great company, indeed. She spat the water into the basin and dried her face, took the mother-of-pearl comb and glided it through her hair until it fall silky around her head. She remembered how they first met in internet, months ago and how fast a very intense exchange had begun, while he still had to be on duty in Iraq. He, the soldier and she, the German woman. Who had thought that they ever would meet in real and who could have expected that they found a deep and fulfilled love, enjoying their frank attitude concerning sex and fantasies, always ready and willing to fulfill each others pleasures. She was longing for being able to be herself, just being woman, just letting herself fall. He made her feel wanted from the first seconds. Alone their chats have been special from the beginning, but she would never forget when they met first. The moment she opened the door, downstairs from the house and thought: "Wow, he is looking damned good" and when he stepped in and they hugged and started to kiss as if they just celebrated a coming home and not a meeting first. It was so great. She smiled while she put her favorite lotion on her face and throat, rubbed it on her breasts and arms, down her belly, her butt and her legs. He loved her body and she enjoyed so much being able to have her kilos, knowing that he enjoy to hold her big butt while gliding into her. She closed her eyes and remembered the excitement when he was sitting in front of her, while they drank a glass whine together. How she was nervous and feeling good the same time, watching every single of his movements until he stood up and draw her with him, starting to dance with her to a music of desire only their bodies could feel. She remembered how her legs felt so weak that she thought she would faint in his strong arms, so overwhelmed from his manly charisma. Not that she ever fainted easily but it was all so unreal and happened the same moment in her life. And then his touches, knowing, absolutely knowing her as if they had shared pleasures already for a very long time. His voice leaded her, comforted her and all his moves, the beautiful play of his muscles, the timbre of the whispered words and his tender touches where leading her to the sweetest excitement. He bent her over, opening her legs from behind and starting to lick her. She moaned with pleasure, excited to feel the way he would treat her body. He continued to please her, then turned her round on the bed to continue playing with her clit, using his fingers now, while kissing her mouth, her throat and her nipples. The way he touched her, gentle but demanding made her come so fast that she was surprised herself. But he gave no peace. He knew from their chats and little web cam plays that she was very well able and longing for multi-orgasms. So he just changed the way of his touches and dived into her pussy, massaging her g-spot with his fingers, while the thumb still rubbed her clit. She was all wet now and while he kissed her again, he felt how she tried to move away, as if she wanted to escape his touches. But he knew her from their chats and smiled deep inside about her playfulness and those little challenges she needed. She was no weak woman, in fact, she was strong and had a strong will too, but for him as trained as he was, it was too easy to hold her down and give her what she needed. The feeling of his power, of his muscles, of being hold, save, comforted and kind of overmastered the same time. She purred and moaned under his treatment, smiling happy and enjoying her pleasures until he let her come another time. He turned her round again, starting to put gel on her butt. It was time to show her what she wanted him to teach her. They had prepared that moment very careful and so, using enough gel, he slowly and tender glided into her anal hole with one finger, very slowly while his other hand still pleased her vulva. The anal muscles where relaxed from the orgasms and she trusted him so much that it was easy for her to open towards him. He left her time until she got used to the feeling. Slowly circling with his fingers he tried to find her hidden points of lust. She was surprised how good it felt. "It does not hurt, you make it so good" she whispered and felt her body shivering from desire when he pushed the finger in her anal hole against her pussy, while his fingers there pressed tender direction anus. She was surprised about the waves of lust through her body. "I want to feel you now" she said. "I am ready for you". He had not expected that so quickly even if he knew that she had tried out that zone since their first conversations about that possibility. She was so open and curious. He always was looking for somebody as crazy in trying out fantasies as himself. And now she was there, bent over, laying on her knees and opening totally towards him, trusting him to give her pleasure, not pain. He wanted to do her good. He took enough gel and put it all over his penis and around her hole again. He opened her anus again very gently with his finger and placed the gel inside, carefully moving. Her excitement grew and she wanted so much to feel him now, even expecting a bit pain. But the more astonished she was, when there was no pain. He just opened her butt so softly with his two fingers and glided with his wonderful penis into her butt - just a bit. Then a bit more, while he waited and let her time to feel. "Oh" she could only say, totally surprised that there was no pain at all, but instead a number of pleasant sensations. Very unexpected. One moment she remembered another experience with someone who was neither careful nor knowing and had caused her so much pain that she was jumping away without ever feeling the wish to try that out again. But now, there was just that feeling of trust. That feeling that nobody would ever come as near as he with his care for her. Deeper he glided into her butt while his hand still touched her clit and pussy and his voice made sure that she was feeling comfortable. She moaned and could not wait longer, pressed herself against him until he glided deep into her. Then they moved. While he wanted still to move careful and slowly, she was already so aroused that she moved harder so he started to rub her clit while gliding in and out, back and forward to a wilder rhythm. She seemed to be totally surprised about the sensations which ran through her body and indeed it was a totally different feeling compared with those feelings she knew. When she orgasmed, it came so hard and unexpected that she shouted from lust. It was a number of waves who seemed to start from different points of her body and she nearly brake down under him, knocked off her knees but always hold from his strong and tender arms. She was shivering but he was holding her, smiling at her, while she smiled back, enjoying the fact that both had come in the same moment. While enjoying his tender touches she felt a deep gratefulness for being shown a new world of possibilities to find pleasure. They kissed until they fall into sleep. She opened her eyes, feeling a bit confused to find herself still leaning against the basin. "I am always daydreaming, since I met him." she thought. She took a bit more from "Hypnotic poison" and with a knowing smile she left the bath, ready to share the next pleasures with him. All was silent, she heard no move. She felt a growing excitement, feeling that he was playing with her. She made silent steps along the floor, trying to get a view through the glass window of the bed-room door, when suddenly he jumped out of the kitchen on the right side, caught her, blindfolded her eyes with a silk shawl and leaded her so gentle to the next surprise of lust.

Chapter 4: Oily Intermezzo

He had lead her with blindfolded eyes into the warm room. Everything was prepared, just she had no idea what was expecting her. Her nude skin was shining already from the lotion she just had used and he loved to smell her body. But now he wanted to show her some new sensations and smiled already because he knew, whatever he does, she would love it. It was sweetness to watch her face, looking with this mixture of cute nosiness of a child and the longing of a woman. He lead her further to the bed and made her lay down. "Uh, that is cold" she said, when she found herself on a plastic foil but he came aside her, already as nude as her and brought the bottle of oil from the side. Slowly he started to drop it all over her body, while his warm hands rubbed it over her skin, warming her up. She smiled and obviously enjoyed the experience. He used more until she was shining from head to toes, then added more oil and dispersed it also between her legs, around her clitoris, vulva and butt hole. She moved into his hands, pressing herself against him, purring like a cat. He smiled, rolled her over and rubbed his penis all over her back, gliding forward and backward while they exchanged oily hugs, slipping through each others fingers, laughing and enjoying the same time. He rubbed upwards and downwards, deeper over her big butt and finally glided into her pussy. She was longing for him and wet as usual, this time mixing her wet juices with the vegetable oil he had used. Her hips made circles and he pushed her, while she was too slippery to be hold. It aroused him even more and he came back to her butt, gliding with his penis now careful into her butt hole. She was used to this in the mean time and enjoyed to have more varieties of pleasure through him. But oily, he was gliding so easy forward and backward, that they both went crazy and wild until they came and he fall on her back, folding his arms around her and protecting her softly until their both breaths went calmer. After a little brake she made him turn round and pleased him until he came into her mouth. They hugged and kissed until they decided to take a shower together to remove oil and foil and enjoy cuddling and spooning in the warmed up bed. They cleaned each others skin, still smiling about the experience and slipped happily pleased under their covers. She pressed her nude body against his wonderful hazelnut brown, nude skin, enjoying once again how perfect their body fitted. While listening to his soft and tender words she found the tiredness come over her and finally slept, being hold and comforted through his arms.

Chapter 5: Fertile Rite

Leaving the field of ancient hill graves behind them they followed the hidden path deep into the woods. The sun shone warm and there was a very soft wind touching their skins. The air was filled with the promise of re-awaking nature and the various songs of the wood birds. Hand in hand they walked further, smiling at each other and enjoying the brightness of this day. He carried a rucksack, filled with a cooled Prosecco and some tasty finger foods, while she had a blanket under her arm. "There we have to go, you see the outer walls of the old Celtic wall?" She showed him the still visible opening of the north gate, even overgrown now from all those centuries who had followed history. But still impressing how much was left from that place. "That is because people do not know it, you can still see the pieces of oblation pots, and burned bones from animals. When you walk east, you come to the point where you see the two rivers flowing together down the valley, which explains the sacred place and why it was chosen. Hidden, difficult to conquer and those holy

31

surroundings." The Celtic wall was one of the bigger ones who had really saved as an outer wall to protect a big community. The names of villages and streets, places and locations around still reminded to the special history of the area. The sun was shining warmer now and even reached the ground of the forest. Near the place of those old given oblations, they found a tiny clearance, where one of those past storms had chopped down some trees and left a little sunny ground with grass, moss and soft tender ground. They smiled and chose that place for their little wood picnic, unfolding the blankets and sitting down in the midday sun. Totally undisturbed, only surrounded by the beautiful twitter of the birds, they cuddled and started to undress, to feel each other nude, her white skin shining above his beautiful hazel brown, her soft and tender fingers gliding with love over his muscles and his erotic manly body. She loved to feel his strength and his stomach and was content that his was not meager. She loved to have something between her hands – and with him it looked extremely great because of his trained body – it was so pleasant to watch his moves, the play of his muscles when he made his very specials moves who reminded her always to a Tiger, who moved with the awareness of the surrounding, the elegance of those wild cats of prey and the enormous strength they have. Being able to be dangerous as well as tender – that was he for her. To her tender and soft, caring and loving as a man can be, but she knew he has been soldier and in war for many years. But now he deserved his peace - and peace and desire was something they loved to share. She too had a rough time behind her, so very early in their relation they found to a silent agreement and understanding. "What is in your mind, baby?" he asked like he often did and as often she answered "Just enjoying the moment" because that was the truth. She felt so aware of every single second with him, feeling his gentle touches and enjoying his company. The day was simply great. He opened the Prosecco and they drank it out of little bowls, while sitting as close as possible, she leaning her head against his throat, he one arm around her. Her body was soft too, far away from being meager and the late pregnancy had left her traces, but he loved her softness and curves, loved to feel her longing and how happy she snuggled against his skin, always open for his longing and always playful enough to animate him too. It was so great to have no fears, no limits, no taboos – just avoiding pain. They agreed to that point. They loved it both, giving and receiving pleasures – no space for pain. Life can be painful enough but they wanted to enjoy their little islands and shared those needs. He brought the bottle into the shadow of a hollowed tree nearby and came slowly back again. The tiger, she thought, feeling aroused while watching him coming near. Even in the forest he is walking without making sound, like avoiding the attention of enemies or avoiding a victim to run away – in that case just avoiding the beautiful atmosphere to fade. He knew her desire for him and enjoyed that too. She laid back and opened her legs, moving her hips teasing while smiling like a little devil. He smiled back and laid down on her. She loved that. In the beginning he always tried not to be too heavy but she loved the comforting feeling of all his weight, of his nude body on her nude skin. They kissed. It was so great to enjoy undisturbed time, no need to hurry. They kissed and wandered up and down each others body until they changed position and he started to lick her clit and labia while she opened her mouth around his penis. Pleasure for both, even she always found it hard not to loose control under his knowing touches. She loved when he licked her and he made it so patient until he knew she had her pleasure and fulfillment. But she took all her effort not to fall too early into those tension which made her impossible to focus on him and tried to give him the maximum pleasure as well. They started slowly but soon fall into a kind of rage, getting crazy for each other, being aroused through the excitement of the other. She clung to him as he grabbed her hips, continuing to eat her out while he started to move up and down in her mouth as well. Her tongue wandered around his shaft, a bit difficult to breath now but she loved to please him with her mouth and feel him getting so hard. And then she was unable to hold it back any longer. Her body had her own life and her back formed a bow while the waves of lust exploded through her abdomen. And while he moaned she felt his sweet, spicy sperm coming down her throat and they hold each other, following the last tensions of their bodies until finally calming down, kissing and holding, laying silent and just holding each other, while the sun warmed their skins and the birds where singing.

Chapter 6: The Hotel Room

The elevator opened. Nobody in that long hotel corridor. She heard her heart beating from excitement. The key showed room 112, so she followed the shown direction. Her steps where more noisy than usual, due to the black shoes she was wearing. They had bought them together for that purpose. Normally she used to wear comfortable walking shoes but that moment she enjoyed the elegance. She was wearing black stockings and a beautiful corsage with black and blue laces, she wear a skirt, top and blue silver blazer but no slip – that was part of their role play. 112. She wanted to knock but then decided to just use the key. Slowly she opened the door. It was dark inside the room. Her hands tried to touch for the light switch, but that moment his arms draw her into the room, one hand stopping her surprised outcry. He closed the door with his leg and pushed her against the wall, kissing her wild. He kissed her neck and throat, and hold her tight with one arm, while he lifted the shirt and just pushed his penis into her hole, knowing her too well and how ready she was for him. He dived into her wetness and heard her moan. She pressed her butt against him and repaid his kisses, longing to feel more of him, longing for his strength and so he gave her the wildness she needed that moment. He fucked her hard until she came but he still left her pressed against the wall. "You remember that restaurant, honey? I promised you a revenge." and with those words he carefully placed a very special tool into her butt, her vagina and placed a third one directly in front of her clit, fixing it all with a special slip. "And now we go to make a little walk." She protested but he showed her a little remote control and turned it on. With a "prrr" the tools started a vibration, he turned it higher until she moaned – and then stopped. "You see, honey, this time, I will control you." He allowed her to rearrange her hair and then they walked. It was difficult for her because she felt so aroused, feeling that tool touching her clit and the power of his control. But she thought he will not really use it in front of others. She knew in the end, he would always protect her. They walked hand in hand to the elevator. It opened and they were alone. They kissed. "Prrr" it started and she moaned while he laughed, obviously enjoying his power.

"You are mean, stop that" she complained but he used the next step until she started to breath harder. Then he released her and stopped. That moment the elevator opened and they let another couple in. He was looking as devilish as she had looked, those few days before in that restaurant. She was scared that he would start the tools right now, but nothing happened. Finally they where alone again and he lead her into a darker corner of the hotel bar. They ordered a little drink and he placed himself in front of her – so she was hidden. Prrr it started and she nearly dropped the glass. He was laughing and just hold her in his arms. "You are really mean." but prrr was the answer and she tried to pass him with the hope to escape to the toilette to remove the tools. "Stop that" she said. "You know, I cannot stay silent." With a very huge grin he started the control again. Prrr in her butt, prrr in her hole and prrr around her clit. Her knees went weaker and she tried to control her moans. He started kissing her. He kissed her harder and pressed his lips on her, while he turned the vibration on maximum. So the few people in the bar recognized an obviously being-in-love-couple, but they had no idea that the woman had one of her strongest orgasms right now, at their side.

They did not see how her legs went weak and how her mate had to hold her, calmed her down and kissed her softly. All they saw was a very caring man who lead an obviously tired or exhausted woman direction elevator. "Are you okay or do you need a doctor" was all they heard. So they had no idea, that the moment the elevator was hiding both from their nosy views, something started to make prrr again. Nobody saw how only few minutes later the man lead the woman to the bed, opening her legs, removing the tools and licking her dry until she came another time. Nobody saw, but – who cares about "nobody"?

Chapter 7: Cinema Movies

Finally a free and undisturbed afternoon. They had so much to do in their works that they were rare – those moments during the days. Even an early evening was something very special and they always used to make the best out of it. Right now they were using their shower together, rubbing each others backs and washing gently every part of their bodies, teasing a bit, pleasing as well, kissing and laughing about their follies. The warm water was running down their bodies and they where short before playing a little shower play, when she saw the watch. "We will miss our movie!" But very hard to interrupt the near and so she just turned round, pressing her butt against his legs while grasping for the towel, which was just fallen on the floor. She felt his strong arms and how he glided inside her, laughing and giving her a little quickie. "Oh, you are bad" she said, too obviously enjoying that. Finally they managed to get dry and into their cloths and hurried grinning down to his car. The cinema was near and they tried to find their places in the half darkness. It was a place in the last row and the rows in front of them where not too filled. All was concentrated to the middle rows of the hall. The commercial stopped the moment, they had find their seats and the movie started. Snuggled into each other arms they enjoyed the near, while laughing about the actors and the funny scenes. Humor combined with brain is a pleasure, the actors where funny and the action exciting. She felt, how he moved away from her, but changing his position to the place right in front of her knee and she was holding her breath. He opened her legs and dived under that wide skirt she was wearing. She gripped the seat harder and felt her heart beating. Oh, he was really mean – but how much she loved that. A short moment of his surprise when he felt that she wear no slip again – and soon she felt his tongue tenderly knocking against her clit. She leaned back. He wandered with his lips and tongue around her lips, slowly up and down, tasting her sweet juices and smiling content about her reactions. It was so easy to please her, she loved his touches so much that she was always wet in his near. He licked and sucked her harder but still slowly. The movie was long enough to enjoy eating her out and to giving things time. He felt her tension, so reduced the intensity, his hands opening her knees as wide as possible, holding her strong as well. He knew she loved that. He also knew her impatience. She wanted him but he had time and enjoyed to play with her needs. So he licked and kissed along her legs, inside down to the knees and back to her Vulva, feeling how she tried to press her against his mouth but he was holding her and played along her other leg. She tried to press his head closer between her legs, but he followed as slowly as possible. Finally he gave in and started to lick her harder. He pressed his mouth over clit and lips than back to the clit, pressed her Venus hill upwards to expose her clit and used his fingers of the other hand to dive into her pussy and into her anal hole. She pressed her arm against her mouth, scared to get noisy and tried to wind herself out of his grip, feeling unable to bear those intense pleasures but now he used more pressure, licked and sucked her harder while diving backwards and forwards into her hole. She bent her back and tried not to moan, but thanks to the loud cinema music, her sounds of pleasure where swallowed and when her legs shivered more and more and her body suddenly bowed under the intense orgasm, she was biting into the cloth of her jacked to hide the shout of lust. He drank her, he licked her and hold her tender, gliding back to his seat in the end. She rolled into his arms and he felt her silent tears of happiness and joy. They kissed and found themselves very surprised when the light went on. The movie was over.

Chapter 8: Bathroom Pleasures

She really missed him so much. Four long weeks had passed without any possibilities to meet. Of course they had called each other, but she awfully missed his company. When she woke up at night, she missed to feel his gentle and comforting hugs, to hear his calm breaths and to feel the warmth of his strong and nude body. She missed their breakfasts together and his smiles. She missed to talk or to laugh, every single moment was so special with him. And she missed their pleasures. Sex with him was like coming home, giving her the playing field and fulfillment she needed so much. She felt a bit sad and disliked that weakness. All would be good soon, she knew he would try everything to get some free days again – but job was job. All that run through her mind, while she undressed in front of the bathroom mirror, letting her blouse glide softly from her white shoulders. She watched herself and wandered with her hands along her cheeks, touched her lips, wandered down her throat and deeper to her breasts, touching gentle her pink nipples, who soon started to look nosy into the air, like little antennas. She imagined his touches and started to undress. She needed him! Her body needed his touches. It was all tension in her, longing and life. She needed to let the tension go!

A view to the boiler told her, it would be enough hot water, so she started to fill the bathtub, added a wonderful smelling bath flagrance and glided slowly into the hot water. That was a feeling. She loved it and was happy being able to do her something good. She brought the shower and removed the head, then changed the water to a very soft rest, strong enough, warm enough and gentle enough the same time.

She closed her eyes and leaned back on that pillow of foam. Her hand guided the water upwards her lips, around her clit. She remembered their chats, she remembered his touches, his mouth, the unique way he loved to please her and while the water started to arose her, she imagined his lips and his tongue. She opened her leg and tried to bring herself more into tension. The other hand pressed against the Venus hill and brought the clit into more exposition. She was already erected and swollen from lust, being further aroused from the water. The tension increased. Then with a sudden wave came the orgasm, shaking her legs through and through, while her body bowed by itself and she made a loud moan of pleasure. But she needed more and few moments later started to bring the water back to the area of lust again.

She felt the next wave coming when there was suddenly an arm around her, holding her straight, while another arm brought the shower away and now leaded the water to her, pleasing her. She was so surprised and shocked in the first moment, but a kiss had comforted her, while floods of happiness ran through her soul. He was there! he was finally back home. And now he made her come and after she found herself shaking inside his arms, he helped her out of the bathtub, dried and kissed her and pushed her right into their air bed. He quickly undressed and opened her legs with his hands, starting to lick her until she came under his tongue. Then he turned her round and brought her to her knees while gliding into her pussy, holding her and taking her soft, first so soft and slowly until he felt his own needs and pushed harder now. She moved her hips and made little circle, he was holding her with his strong hands and listened to her moans again. Her wet hair was flowing over her back and she started to feel the tension again. He felt how her muscles contracted and then stronger and finally he felt how her pussy closed in contractions around his penis. He had to let it go and still, was longing for all of her. She knew it, she grabbed the gel at the side of her bed and placed it around her butt, tried to get his penis and added gel there too. He helped her and then touched so gently her butt hole, gently, so soft. He knew how to cause no pain and she was longing to feel him.

And so he was gliding tender into her, so tender that she was overwhelmed from her love and his care. He wanted to give her time but she wanted him to come now too and started to move wildly, bringing him inside as deep as possible. It was such a wonderful feeling, so totally unexpected. She trusted him blind and knew, he would always take care, thus she was able to open to him and now, making wild moves, all she wanted was him to ejaculate in her.

He finally could not hold it anymore and enjoyed the feeling to come right into her small hole. Still connected, they laid down, holding each other in a very close hug.

Then he carefully removed his penis, turned her round in his arms and kissed her. They just kissed and hugged. Then he smiled to her: "I came in the right moment, honey." Her happy and satisfied smile was all the answer he needed.

Chapter 9: Playing Cop

Her grin was wide, while she placed a number of baking powder packets with stripes on her nude body. He used the time to slip into his cops uniform, grinning himself – two big kids going for a little extra play. She chose a little silk "nothing" and stockings, red shoes and a red wig, chose a very shrill make up and started a little cat walk along her floor. He came from the dining room, which was supposed to be his office. "You again" he said with a very strict face. "I told you to stay away from my quarter, we do not want prostitutes here nor dealers. Hands against the wall and legs wide." "Let me in peace and go your way" she said stubborn, trying to get the other way, but he grabbed her and pressed her against the wall. "Pray that I do not find drugs again!" he hissed and hold her with one of his strong arms, while his hands wandered along her body. He touched the first hidden powder. "Damned, what's that! I told you, there will be no mercy, when I ever get you again with this stuff. This time you go to jail." "No please, leave me alone. It is just this one little packet for myself." she begged, but he

49

continued the examination. His hand wandered down her stomach and found the next packet. "So what is that?" he shouted. "You come right into my office now!" She tried to run away and fight him, but he hold her tight and pressed her into his office. "Undress!" "No, please!" she begged, but he was in rage. "Undress or I tear those cloths from your body!" "No, please let me go!" but he was strict and started to bring her top away. "Tell me honest, do you have more hidden stuff?" "No, I don't have more, please let me go one more time!" she begged, looking close to tears. "Oh stop that, this will not help you this time!" He removed her skirt. "Damned, what is that! Another two?" He found the rest of the hidden powders and turned her round against the table. "You think, you can lie to me? I will teach you a lesson." he said and opened his trouser. "Don't dare that!" she shouted. "You still have not enough?" he asked and glided into her pussy. "Then get this here!" and he started to fuck her hard. She tried not to show her pleasure and hided her grin. Role play is role play, so she played to dislike it and asked for mercy, but he was really not willing to give in this time. "You will stay in this jail until you are getting a saint! And you will do what I tell you, else you stay here even longer!" "No please, let me go! I can find a real job and make something out of my life. This time, I will not go for drugs again, promised!" He stopped to move and told her to knee in front of him. "And now you lick me, than I will think that over." So she obeyed and started to play with him the way he liked. She danced with her tongue around his shaft and head, sucked and used her lips and tongue, the whole mouth, while touching him also with gel, which she brought on her hands, to make all more slippery. He grunted content and hided his smile. Hard to play strict when he just wanted to hold her in his arms, so he remembered his role and pressed her head down, well taking care not to hurt her. He gave her the rhythm he needed and finally gave in, let his sperm run into her mouth, while she sucked him dry and tenderly hold him in her arms. "Come baby, the floor is cold." he whispered and helped her up, brought her to the bed and tenderly covered her with the blankets, pressing her so close against his body. That was good, just to hold her and she smiled so happy, leaning her head against his breast. "I love you" he told her. "I love you too" she smiled.

Chapter 10: Looking For a New Job

She was wearing her business dress, black blazer, black top, black trouser , her long hair very neat and strict looking, cool and distant business make up – looking like one of those women, who seem to have eaten a citron for breakfast or to think, smiling is something, which has to be done in secret. She placed her laptop on the table, now this was her office. There was a knock at the door. "Come in" she said, trying hard not to grin. Damned that was difficult. He saw it and was one moment tempted to make her laugh, but he was to nosy what she had planned in her role. "Sit down" she ordered, looking very tough and arrogant. "So Mr. Smith, you think you bring the right qualifications for this job?" "Yes" he said, "I am sure about it." "It doesn't matter if you are sure, you have to convince me. So, tell me about your past jobs, what you did, about your qualifications and goals in life, which time you could start, your personal situation and if you are willing to travel." He started to give her a little overview over his curriculum vitae, being interrupted here and there from her questions. "So, why do you think, I should chose you and not your business rivals? What do you think, you may have or do, what others cannot do as well?" "I can eat you out until you faint" he answered, deciding to take the play over. "Well" she said "That is the minimum qualification. You must know we will test our candidates before we make our decisions..." she hesitated. He smiled. "Ok, Mr. Smith, you show now, if that is all only empty swaggering, or if you really have your little extra talents." She stood up and went to the massage chair, where she undressed the trouser, opened her legs – wearing no panty, so just being as nude as new born. "Eat me out and make sure that you do your job good. Afterward I will think about a contract as my personal assistant - maybe. That depends on you, Mr. Smith. Now start!" She lasciviously laid back and allowed him to knee between her legs. He opened her thighs as far as possible and started to touch her labia softly with his tongue. He knew her impatience and played with her. And really, she tried to press her against his mouth. He smiled and opened her labia with his tongue, carefully pushing them aside, wandering along the swollen pink flesh of her vulva. She tasted sweet like a sin. He dived into her hole, playing deeper inside her and touching for those points she loved so much. He watched her face. She had closed her eyes and looking content and relaxed, her hands shivered a bit from excitement, a pleased smile on her lips. She could not play Mrs. Tough with him. He wandered with his tongue higher to her clit, circling around and pressing his lips on it, sucking a bit and rubbing it with his tongue. He dived into her pussy with his fingers, while his other hand draw her skin a bit away, direction navel. Now the clit was erected and waiting for his treatment. He started to suck and lick it faster, trying to keep up the necessary pressure, while using his fingers as well. He heard the moaning and felt the shiver of the thighs. "Yes, love, continue" she whispered, forgetting her role play, just giving in into his touches. He went on, increasing his pressure on her, while she started her tries to move away from him. Her little challenges, the power games, she needed, so he hold her tight and continued to lick her, to suck her and press his mouth on her until she suddenly bowed with all her body and a moan escaped, while the same moment he felt her liquid running out of her pussy. He licked her dry and enjoyed the thought to let her just a little brake before the next demonstration of his abilities. She gently touched his head, caressed his hair and whispered "You have the job."

Chapter 11: The Massage Chair

He was so tired after the long travel. It really have been some hard weeks, so she made him relax in the massage chair, turning on the vibrations and the heating of the seat. It was not planned, but he fall into a nap and she covered him warm and smiled. Good that he finally found a bit peace, she thought. She went back to kitchen, prepared some little finger food and brought their favorite liqueur wine – Maphrodaphne. Blood red and looking like the incarnation of sin. She decorated the table and placed the food and glasses, the servicing, the candles, then turned on the Temptations CD, not loud, just as comforting background music. She sat down on their bed, watching him. Then she drank half of her glass wine, while reading a book. One hour later she found it time to go for a little action and while he slept, she opened his trouser and freed his wonderful manhood. "There you are." she whispered and brought her mouth around his penis, which was still soft and relaxed, but soon, after she started to make her usual dances, he felt the growing stiffness. That turned her on. She felt getting wet herself, while she continued to lick and suck him. From that pleasant treatment he woke up and smiled. Yes, that was how he loved to wake up and that was what he really had missed those past weeks. He let her do her job a while then told her to turn round. He wanted to see her butt, so she did that and bent over the foot chair of that massage unit, while he came to his knees and brought his penis into her butt hole, using the gel she had placed in their near. He loved to glide slowly into her and wanted to stay calm a while to make her used to the feeling, always taking care not to give her the slightest pain. So they did not move, but where suddenly aware of the vibrations of their massage chair, which just changed automatically into those harder pushing vibrations which went through and through their bodies. They where surprised. So while they felt those little pleasant shock waves running through and through, they were turned on so much that she started to feel those inner contractions and could not hold herself back any longer. She moved her hips, wiggled her butt and moved herself in the tact to those massage pushes, what was so arousing that he could not hold back either. They came together and fall moaning from the chair. He saved her from a hard landing, but hold her tender, while she rolled on his stomach, looking down on him with that relaxed smile, he loved so much. They kissed and continued sixty-nine until they came again. "That was a delicious sweet appetizer, let's go to drink some wine" he whispered into her ear. They brought the finger food and wine near their bed and enjoyed to eat the little specialties from each others bodies. The wine was sweet and strong, they leaned against each other, drinking and toasting on lifelong love.

Chapter 12: Tell Me Your Dream, Honey!

He woke up from her moves and was watching her face. It was for sure no night mare, because she was smiling in her dream, then moving again, moving her hips and turning round. After a while she moved back, snuggling against his body and was silently moaning. He watched her, touching her face very gently. She was definitely looking cute. He glided tender over her hard nipples, making little circles around them with his fingers. Whenever he did that, she started to give a kind of purring sound, unimportant how deep she slept and he loved to do so. It worked again and he smiled. She turned again into his direction and her arm wandered around his body, hugging him close in her sleep. He was holding her, breathing her hair, the flagrance she loved to use and the lotion of her body, also the smell of the shared lust. So he found back to sleep and both did not move until few hours had passed by. He woke up when she came back to bed, obviously after a walk with the dog. She was so cold that he just hugged and warmed her until her skin warmed up and she stopped to shiver.

The weather was still so icy and those days had been really windy. She pressed her nude body against him, enjoying his warmth, the feeling of his body and smiled with that so typical content impression. "So tell me your dream honey" he whispered softly in her ear. "It seemed to be something pleasant." "Oh yes, it was so amazing, so wild and free. First I saw us, climbing around that hill where I showed you another old sacred place with a tiny hidden Celtic wall, then you suddenly wanted to show me how to catch a fish with your hands – and while I turned round, you caught a big one. It was still living and slippery. You wanted to tease me and hunted me with that fish, while I squeaked laughing and tried to run away, but I slipped and the fish tried to jump on me. In the end we rolled over each other." "The fish and you?" "No, you and I, the fish was gone, but we were laughing, it was so ridiculous and silly, we just laughed and played around like kids, forgetting the world. And then my dream changed, I was riding an elephant but he was running as fast as a racing car while you followed with a galloping wild horse, a very huge one. I was laughing because I was riding your elephant and it was faster than your horse. So I enjoyed how you was hunting behind me. We had so much fun, just being so speedy and the next scene we just have been on the top of a monster wave. There was no skate board, just we with our bare feet. The power of the water drove us higher and forward in such a speed, there was so much life in my dreams. It was just that feeling of living life without limits, with liberty, joy and that great feeling to fly with the elements. Then we just laid down there in the warm sand. It was a beach, totally protected from intruders, just we had our secret place there and there you started to please me with your mouth. It was so intense that I felt it through and through and suddenly you turned me round, dived into my hole and we were jumping in slow motion like being on the moon but those jumps while we have been connected where so pleasant and we came with a number of orgasms." "Wow, amazing. You should write that down, baby." "Oh, who would be interested to read such strange dreams?" "Who knows, they are special somehow. You should make a book out of this all, maybe it is an inspiration for other lovers, to please each other and share joy." "Well, I will see, maybe I will write it down. But now I want to enjoy you again. Please do it for me." "How do you love it now, honey?" "First I want to lay down like princess and just feel you, how your tongue and mouth and lips arouse me, play with me, but then I want to feel all of you and this morning I would love it laying sidewards and moving so slowly. I am in a very tender and soft mood." "Hmmm, sounds very good to me." He kissed her nose and smiled to her, kissed her lips and started to wander with his mouth along her throat, her breasts, staying and playing again with her nipples and then deeper and deeper to that nosy little clit, who was impatiently waiting for another pleasant treatment. He touched her with his tongue, just a little touch, playing with her again. Then brought his mouth around the clit, not moving, not pushing, only letting her feel the warmth of his breath like an embrace. Then his tongue touched her again but a bit longer, while he draw the skin above a bit higher and started with more intense touches. She gave sounds of joy, moving her hips and pressing herself against him. She wanted him, she wanted him to increase his touches, but he took his time, to built up more tension. He wandered deeper and tasted her juices, dived deep into her hole with his tongue, enjoying the sweetness, then slowly licked back upwards to her clit. He repeated that several times, licking her lips as well, then stayed around her clit and started to lick her harder and more intense. She bowed her body and tried to move but his grip was strong, tender and strong and while his arms opened her leg wide, he went on to lick her until she went wild under his mouth. He knew her already to know her signs, the shaking muscles of her legs, the mourning, the deeper sounds of pleasure and he went on, more and more intense until her body reared up powerful and she came so hard. He was holding her, touching her gently, allowing her a little rest. She breathed hard and was still shaking from pleasure, so he hugged her, while she put her arms around him. Her eyes closed, she was laying there, smiling like a kid in a candy store. He softly turned her sidewards and brought his hard penis between her legs, touching for the entrance of her cave. She was so hot there and wet, he glided into her while she pressed her hips against him. It was difficult, not to follow the impulse to take her wild and bring himself the ease he was longing for now. But he wanted to please her and give her time to built up another orgasm. So they first just laid that way, barely moving, then it was she who started to move more intense and he smiled. She was so greedy for pleasures. He had always wished that, to be just able to follow needs without thinking, and without the fear that it could be too much for the partner. Whatever nonsense came into his mind, she was there, willing to play the ideas and came by herself with further fantasies, so they had plenty of possibilities, even if sometimes they also enjoyed the good old sex. He felt the beginning pain from holding his needs back and she felt his tension. "It is your turn, love." she whispered, "give yourself ease, I am fine." She pressed her butt against him and even if he was warmed up and hot between her legs, around her back and arms, her butt was cold and it turned him on to feel that mixture of hot and cold skin, so when she started to move her hips he started to move faster until he felt the near explosion. But he had managed to touch her clit with one hand and that double pleasing made her come just seconds before him. He felt the shaking of her legs and how she reared up again. That was too much. He came too and felt that big ease and relaxation of his body. They hugged and spooned, feeling so good and near until he heard her breath. She was sleeping in his arms like a kid. He covered her and hold her as tight as possible, kissing her neck and her hair. For a while he was enjoying the near and thought about this peaceful place where he felt welcome from the first moment. They have been strangers who decided to meet and became lovers. Fate is something great. And while remembering the first moments together, he found smiling back to a little nap.

Chapter 13: The Secret of the Wild Blue Chicory

From June to August, the dam along the Danube river is full of wild, blue chicories. The beauty of those flowers and their sweet smell is inviting thousands of butterflies. They walked along the stony path, enjoying the beauty of nature. "You know that flower? It was me, waiting for you." She smiled. "There is a legend around it, well, there are several myths, but one is that there was a woman with blue eyes. She was in love with a soldier who had to go far away into another country. She stood there on this way, waiting and waiting for him, day and night, while her tears where running. She waited so long that her father was scared for her and told her to forget that man and to make her heart free for another love. But she wanted nobody else – so in the end, a god was feeling pity and bewitched her into that flower. Only the color of that plant is reminding to the wonderful blue of her eyes. So she can only be released through the kisses of her love. He is the only one on this earth to set her free." "And why is this you?" "Because I had to wait so long, and it was only your kiss I wanted, your touch I was longing to feel. I even have those blue eyes and you are a soldier. It fit's perfect. So, release me now." He took her tender in his arms and kissed her, forgetting the world around him. The daylight was bright but they seemed to be the only wanderers in the middle of this beauty. They walked away from the path and laid down into the little paradise of flowers and high grass, kissed and didn't care about anything else. She wear her skirt and while he opened her legs he felt that once again, she was wearing no underwear. The wetness between her legs was too much to bear. He quickly opened his trouser, gave the area a last check and then dived into her warm, wet cave. Soft and tender he made her forget the long weeks alone, the longing which had to wait, the lonely nights and how much she had missed him. Tender he moved out and in, slowly but passionate and she moved her hips, hugging and kissing him. When she came he stopped to control himself and let his sperm flow, holding her careful in his strong arms, like a jewel. No words necessary, they just looked into each others eyes and her blue eyes where shining with that amazing glow he loved to watch so much. As he loved her smile.

"Did I release you, honey?" "You saved me right in time, love." They stayed laying in their embrace, they saw people coming closer, but still far enough away, so they rearranged their dresses and just sat there, side on side, watching the river flow.

Chapter 14: Handcuffed

He took a nap on their massage chair. His breast moved under his evenly breathes. She was watching him for a while and decided to let him sleep. So about one hour passed, while she took a bath and enjoyed a glass of sweet red whine. After she wear her black lingerie, she softly touched his arm. But he was still sleeping so deep. A little devilish thought came into her mind and silently she was looking for silk shawls in her wardrobe. She found only three but thought, they will do, then came slowly and very silent near to the chair. She started to fix his left arm at the backrest, then waited a moment, but his pupils still moved under his eyelids and showed her his estate of dreaming. So she took the other shawl and fixed his right arm, gently but straight enough. The longest shawl she had left for his legs. They were high on that foot chair and so the decided to whirl the shawl around both legs, then round the chair and made a knot. Content with the result, she lighted some candles and drank another half glass red wine, then slowly came back to him and pulled down the comfortable sport trouser he was wearing. He grunted and moved his head, but was still sleeping. With a grin, she draw the trouser down to his knees, she had done the same with one grip with his underwear, so now he was laying half nude in front of her. She bent down to him, and started to take his penis into her mouth. It was still sleeping, but after she licked it a while, she found herself very pleased with the result. That was the moment he woke up and wanted to touch her – but no chance. She giggled when he tried to free his hands but continued to please him. The next devilish thought came into her mind, so she turned round, climbed over his legs, showing him her butt and touched his penis with her vulva just a tiny bit. He tried to move his hips higher, but was fixed too good on that chair, so he could not dive into her. She continued teasing him, bent over that chair and allowed him to see, how she was touching herself, knowing it would drive him crazy. "Come down to me, baby, let me feel you." he whispered but she continued to wiggle her butt, to tease him, to play with herself, lick him in between and was planning to continue that game for a while longer, when suddenly he grabbed her and pressed her down on his penis. She squealed from glee but the same time a bit shocked that he had managed to free both hands without her recognizing that. She tried to escape laughing, but that moment, he freed already one leg and while he hold her tight with one arm, he freed the other leg, laughing about her tries to escape him and his sweet revenge. "Okay baby, nice try. You know what I will do with you now?" "Kissing me and telling me, I am the best?" she laughed. "I will fix you now and have my little play with you. Look what I have for you." But before he pushed her a bit with his penis, a bit wild but did not allow her to come. He was so horny now but he staid inside her, while he moved her forward to his bag and brought some handcuffs from there. Then grabbed her with that arm, while he took the covers from the bed with the other, draw them on the floor and laid her down, on her stomach. "So baby, how do you like that?" he laughed, fixing her arms with the handcuffs on the heavy table legs. Then he took one of her shawls and fixed her one leg at the big desk and the other at the furniture for books. So she was spread wide and had no chance to move away. She tried to free herself as well but his binding was strong. She could not see what he was up to, heard him using the fridge, heard him picking up something from her commode, and then his steps back to her. He undressed, slowly and obviously enjoying the situation. Then she felt, how he brought gel between her labia and around her butt hole. The next moment she felt something ice cold in her pussy. He was putting two little round ice cubes into her. "And now let's see how this feels" he said and slowly entered her with his stiff phallus. It was arousing to feel that mixture out of her hot wetness combined with those icy cubes and he fought the impulse back to let himself fall into pleasure and just give in... not so fast. He wanted to have his fun now and enjoyed the teasing. She wanted more, she was ready for him and tried to hold him with her muscles, what made it an extra sweet feeling. He brought her little tools and one of the big pillows which he stiffed under her hips to expose her bottom. Then he pushed one of those vibration eggs – the longer one - directly into her pussy, while he pressed the other tender but demanding against her clit. She moaned, being nearly unable to cope with the expected pleasures. He turned those vibrators on, slowly increasing. More. She moaned and moved her hips. More. She was breathing harder now, building up the tension. He added more gel around her butt hole, feeling the tension himself now. He wanted to come. He stuck his penis into her butt hole, gliding easily into her, and more, maximum while he just took her now, knowing she would love it. Then he felt her coming, all her muscles contracted. He could not hold it any longer and eased himself, turning the vibrator off, while her muscles still contracted and her legs were shaking. He hugged her a little while, then slipped down between her legs. The pillow still exposed her while her legs was spread. He saw her liquid and licked her dry, while she enjoyed that feeling. He knew what she desired and licked her clit, while he brought the vibration eggs into her two holes. This time he made the maximum at once and she moaned from pleasure and excitement. He licked her greedy and enjoyed that she came as quick as a rocket. He turned the tools off. Then he remembered her teasing and made her come a third time, the vibrator against her clit and enjoying her butt hole again, this time all slowly and with enough time to come again. When he felt her contractions, he left her a little brake, removed the shawls and handcuffs, turned her round and just hold her in his arms. She looked like a kitten who drank milk, smiling content and pleased. They kissed. No words necessary. A long while later they showered and dried each other, laid down under the covers – this time on the more comfortable bed and enjoyed together the sweet red wine. "How did you manage to escape?" she asked. He smiled. Some secrets she did not need to know. "But you obviously enjoyed the revenge, honey." "Hm, I should tease you more often, when you go for revenge. That is a fine treatment." He laughed. She was definitely looking cute. One moment later, she was fallen to sleep. He draw her nude body against his, covered her and enjoyed the feeling of her curves, her soft skin and how good it felt to have her in her arms. Next moment, he was gone too.

Chapter 15: Another Dream

It was some time now until he was able to get some free days from his work, but she knew he would do his best and wanted to support him. At least it was good that she was used to cope with things alone and was able to live alone without feeling lonely – an art, not too many people are capable. Most people need attraction from themselves and are totally lost when being left alone with their fears, hopes, experiences, thoughts, dreams and especially the evening and night hours. She occupied herself and had several projects running. Ideas for new photo motives. Right now she finished some uploading of the newest shots, changed the rechargeable batteries to prepare everything for the morning and laid her camera back on the table.

No, she was not lonely, but she missed him – and her body was longing for him as well as her soul was longing for his company. She drank a hot cup of herbal tea, took a last evening shower, massaged the wonderful body butter into her skin and finally went to bed, totally nude as usual. The light was off, only those little lamps from the modem and her laptop were blinking. She closed her eyes and started to touch her breast with two fingers, drawing tender circles around her nipples. She was longing for him. Thinking about his voice, thinking about his strength and the way he used to touch her. Thinking about his smile and his kisses and thinking about his tenderness. Her hands went down, deeper down along her navel, down to her clit and separating her lips in a careful play. She circled slowly around the inner lips, diving a bit in the wetness and circling tender up to her clit. She wanted to please herself to find some ease but she felt so tired, that sleep came over her, before she fulfilled her needs. The night hours passed. She slept deep and undisturbed. She dreamed about water, clear and warm water – no basin, no pool, she was examining it. It was a lake, a lake full of warm and soft crystal clear water. She saw beautiful colored fishes gliding through the underwater-world. She developed plants and corals, and stones in red and blue, green and yellow. It was the most beautiful combination of colors she had ever seen. She went deeper and started to swim, feeling joy in her heart and free, not burdened from sorrow, but with the happy innocence of a child who is astonished watching its surroundings. Some of the fishes came nearer and allowed her to touch them tender and she dived happily under water to follow them, being aware of the fact that she was able to breath here as well. So she explored the sea, dived deeper and deeper, always surrounded from light and beauty. A big coral rock was right in front of her, it was bigger than those others and overcrowded with crystals, glowing and sparkling. She was impressed and utmost happy to find such a treasure. So she swam nearer, touched its surface and examined its sides, when she developed an opening, as big as a window. Curious she dived through it and found herself inside a warm and beautiful cave. In spite of the fact that it was under water, there was a hidden light source which dived the cave into a very soft reddish light. There was no water inside that cave, only a tiny pool, the rest was dry and warm, very flat and comfortable ground, like marble, but warm. It was like a hidden shelter place, she felt comfortable and free, so protected, knowing with all her senses that there would never be harm. She laid down on the rocks, feeling happy, when she was hugged by strong arms and heard the beloved voice whisper into her ears. "Hey baby, how are you, I miss you." "I miss you too" she said and happily slang her arms around his neck. "Finally" she whispered, kissing him passionately and pressing her nude skin against his body. Without foreplay he started to glide into her and so they just sat together, being connected, being one body. They were not moving, but suddenly they found themselves sitting on the back of a giant sea turtle who carried them away, shaking in the rhythm of her strokes. That rhythm was so arousing that their bodies gave into that pleasure until they came. But it did not end, they were still kissing and connected, when the sea turtle brought them to a secret island and gave them way to a wonderful beach with white, soft sand. Nobody was there, disturbing the lovers. It was like receiving a blessing from an ancient goddess, when the turtle touched their foreheads as a fare well and went back to the sea, because the lake was gone and they found themselves on an island in the middle of the ocean. It was beautiful and warm there and they felt, whatever they would need, it would be there, so they walked along, hand in hand until they stood in front of a huge swing. He sat down and she climbed on him, letting him glide again into her pussy. He started to push the swing and brought them softly but steady higher and higher, so they were flying far over that island, back and fore while she felt her stomach tickle and the tension in her hips again. She was laughing and giggling, being aroused and happy, cheerful and pleased all together, while enjoying his penis inside her and the growing tension. She felt already the contraction of her muscles, while her body had its usual own life. It was as if he would give her vibrations everywhere and she started to moan from pleasure while she felt waves of orgasm shaking her through. That was the moment, she woke up in the middle of the night, feeling her lips swollen and wet from lust and those waves of orgasm for real. She opened her commode for her toys and laid them on her clit while she pushed the dildo softly deep into her pussy. She also took a little anal plug and dived it into the coconut cream. It glided easily into her. Then she turned the vibrators on. She was already so aroused that her body needed only few moments to dive deep into those waves of pleasure. She could not stop, still present was the feeling of having her love inside her, of feeling his strong arms and the connection. So she turned the vibrations on again, and found herself shouting loud, quickly trying to bite into the pillow to avoid too much noise, but she had to do it another time and so, she moved the vibrators just a bit to get another spot of lust and turned them on. This time the clit was already over-sensitive, but she massaged the g-spot and another point, she had developed some years ago and while she did that, the waves of lust seemed to come from another place of her body. Her legs were shaking and she moaned from lust, feeling all those wetness between her. She just laid there, breathing hard but slowly relaxing again, until she needed to cover again and found herself in deepest sleep until the morning, when she woke up with a smile and started happy into her new day.

Chapter 16: Just a Quickie

All dressed and done and good in time, she was contently checking the time. Just – where was he? "Love? Are you ready?" she asked, but no sound. She looked into the kitchen, but nobody there. She looked outside the window, expecting to see him standing aside his car – but nobody there either. "Love?" She walked through the floor and opened their room, nothing. Very confused she turned round but the moment she did that, he jumped from behind the door and grabbed her, she screamed from shock but laughed the same moment. "Hell, you shocked me, you have only nonsense in your head, really!" but he smiled and did not let her go. "Love, we have to go now, stop that!" she grinned and tried to free herself, but the only response she got was to be turned round and bent over the table. He enjoyed that, brought her skirt high and found what he had expected: no underwear. "You are a bad girl again, so what will I do with a bad girl?" He glided into her pussy and gave her some heavy pushes, pressing her down to the table. She moved her hips. "You love that, I know!" he said with a

81

rough voice, but this time it was his turn. He pressed her down and just took her, pleased his needs and for once was only thinking about himself, taking her hard until he came. But she was so aroused from his little "attack" that she came only moments after him, feeling him moving for the last ecstasy when she was able to let go herself, enjoying the wild pushes and being pressed down so demanding. He felt her contractions and smiled. The better ...

Chapter 17: Bondage

She was very excited. Today a totally new experience waited for her and she stood in front of him with a beating heart. It was warm in the room and she had very red cheeks from the sweet red wine they had enjoyed before. His eyes were shining as well, but not only from the wine. He was pleased being able to try an old fantasy. In his arms a long rope was waiting to be used for their first bondage experience and he made her lay down on the soft covers, he had carefully placed on the floor to give her the maximum comfort. He made her knee and lay on her knees like an embryo, while he started to bind and knot the rope around her body, making sure to expose those spots he needed for their common pleasure later. While fixing and binding her, he felt not only aroused but also touched by her trust to give herself into his fantasy, knowing he would never harm or willingly hurt her, would never go too far and never overstep her borders. He wanted to hug and hold her, to let her feel his care, but she knew. He was watching her face from the side. She had closed her eyes, her lips formed to a happy smile. All was good. He tied her to a little packet and tried to get a good mixture of tightness and comfort, trying all the time if it is not too close, to avoid to interrupt her blood circulation. It took some time, like creating a little piece of art. He had many ideas in his mind, but for this time, he wanted her to be a little packet, something he could easily role and move. Finally it was done. She was excited, he saw her wetness between her exposed lips. He bent down to her, starting slowly to lick and taste her holes, to enjoy her, to eat her without urge. She felt waves of lust from his tongue and mouth but also excitement from being totally helpless now, unable to move, to turn, to do anything. All she could was reacting and the same time she loved this because it gave her the possibility to concentrate only on all those sensations he gave her. He loved to lick her and took his time, opening her lips with his hands and diving with his tongue as deep as possible. Then he glided into her, enjoying the power to use her body and give her pleasure while pleasing himself. It was great to see her tight with all those knots and strings. He was content with his work, so slowly moved inside her, while he now started to touch her clit as well. She moaned and tried to move but was totally fixed and helpless. He rolled her on her back and found his way between her lips again, licking her taste and her clit now more intense until she had her first orgasm. He tasted the new, spicy sweet juices and dug his tongue deep inside her pussy, circling inside and enjoying her pleasure and taste. She went ecstatic but again he interrupted, rolled her back on her knees and brought gel around her butt hole and his penis. While he carefully entered her butt, he also brought his fingers into her pussy and around her clit. He started to rub her and it was nearly too much for her to bare when he increased his moves inside her butt, letting her feel his power as well as his tenderness. She was totally wild now, while he took a vibrator and pushed it carefully into her pussy, holding it there while he fastened his moves inside her butt. He already felt her contractions when his other hand brought her massage egg on her clit, turning the vibration already very high. Now he felt that the vagina tried to push the vibrator outside, contracting already, but he was holding it, so it staid inside her, while his other hand fixed the massage egg. This time all her strength was for nothing, she was unable to move so he had it easy to hold all at his place while he moved faster. She came already and contracted hard, but he gave her no rest, even if she told him to give her a little brake now but he knew her too well, so just brought the massage egg a bit more left to the other side of her clit and was holding the vibrator now so, that it spread a bit her entrance of her pussy, then turned both on maximum until he felt her beginning contractions again. He could not hold it any longer so came right into her butt, while she had such a hard orgasm that he felt the vibrator and his own penis being pressed out of her. She was shaking all over her body and breathing very hard. But he turned her round on her back and licked her inner and outer lips another time, enjoying the sweetness of her liquids. After a while he licked higher and closed his lips around her clit. She was oversensitive now and he know, a further treatment there with her tools would be too much for her, but not with his tongue. That softness would be now exactly what could stimulate her another time, but he wanted to add the vibrator and put it back into her pussy, while he brought one of her plugs carefully into her butt, not forgetting to use enough gel on it. It easily glided into her, because she was still open from him, open and wet. He felt her excitement and how she became ready for pleasures again and started to lick her hard, while he turned the vibrations on maximum. She was fighting now against the bondage rope but had no chance to move, so her tension and arousal was nearly unbearable for her, but he licked her so intense until she came another time. He felt the further liquid and licked her dry again, while all her muscles seemed to shiver from orgasm. He sat behind her and was holding the packet like a baby, shaking and holding her softly before he started to remove the rope, giving her the ability to move back. But she was not able to move, being still aroused so much, that her body shivered. He helped her on their bed and covered her warm, holding her pressed against his breasts, kissing her and giving her all she needed. After a while he felt her eyes wander around his face. When he looked at her, he found her smiling. "You liked that, honey?" he asked her. "Yes, so much." "Really? Or was it a bit too long or too much for you?" "No, you can add that into our repertoire, I want to have that more often." He was happy about her pleasure and once again thought, what a luck it is to find somebody as open and longing for pleasures, being crazy and without taboos like himself. They warmed up and enjoyed some more wine, listened to music and enjoyed their love and near. After a while they spoke about the possibilities of bondage. "We could check some pages in internet, maybe we would find something we like." she suggested. "Or we find a good porn magazine and try out all we love." "We can do everything, whatever we love to do." and gave him a kiss. Life was so good!

Chapter 18: The Table

Circumstances had forced the two lovers into another very long distance, where they only had their calls and chats to overcome the time. I tried to find more about what happened, but her notices contained only some clues, plus some missing pages, where she had removed them from her booklet. It was obvious that she had wanted to protect the private sphere of her lover, who had to face some private troubles. I went through the printed emails and decided to leave that story open, but to continue instead with their reunion, about four long months later.

She started an entry about her fears, short before they met again. She wrote about the long time of distance and that she hardly believed that it will finally happen to meet again. It was so long that she had felt his tender touches and somehow, she had felt moments of ice cold fear, if this all may still be real. But whenever those fears came up, she started to breath deep and became aware of those very old wounds and that she had decided to start new, to trust new and so came back to her attitude. It seemed to be hard sometimes to believe into good developments. What if he would change his mind in the last second? But no, not him. She remembered all the dialogues and she tried to calm down. The hours before he arrived had been very difficult for her, more than she ever had told him. She remembered other promises which had been given and how much her trust was betrayed in the past, but then told herself: stop, be able to let all go, that has nothing to do with him. He was different, he was no man of empty promises. He had a rough time himself and could hardly be blamed for circumstances. But she felt that she urgently needed to see his smile, to feel his arms around her to feel that it is still real. She needed him to come.

The night she barely found sleep. One part was happy and full of pleasant anticipation, the other part could not stop to dig into past disappointments and made it very hard for her. The morning came and she decided to believe. She prepared some food and remembered his hugs, his voice. Finally an SMS arrived, where he wrote her to be on the road. That moment, her joy started to flow without those shadows of the past. It will be real, she thought. I will have him back and he did not forget me. She felt the warmth in her soul and felt the happiness brightening her mood. The next hours she spend busy preparing the rooms, the candles and went to buy some wine. Back to her apartment, she took a bath with the scent of wild roses. She closed her eyes and enjoyed, how the water touched her skin. He will touch me here, she thought and started to massage her breasts, following those areas of lust down to her navel, from where she started to tickle herself pleasantly and soft with her nails, while she played with the water around her clit until she decided to give herself a bit relief. The water was warm and massaging her labia. She placed her feet on the basin and tried to bring her hips above the water surface, feeling already the first pleasant waves which always came from that mixture of endeavor and excitation. She now led the water directly on her clit, trying to bring her hips higher again, when she suddenly felt the waves of lust overwhelming her and with a loud moan from deep inside her throat, she felt the orgasm taking control over her body. That was good. She smiled, while she relaxed and prepared herself. Hours passed, he had a long long way, but earlier than expected, she got a call. "I'm in front of your house." With beating heart she wanted to jump down the stairs to greet him, but was so excited and happy that she feared that tears will start to flow and the last she wanted was to greet him with tears. So she stayed upstairs, trying to calm down, to breath deep and regain control over her emotions. Finally she heard his steps. He always had a very special way to walk down or up the stairs. Once again she was thinking about a wild panther or tiger and showers of desire went through her body. There he was, joy over joy when she saw his smile. It is real, she thought. And finally the kiss, his hug and his strong arms holding her tight while she felt how she found peace that very second. He always had that effect on her, his presence seemed to be the magic she needed to calm down and find peace, while feeling lively and aroused the same moment. They went to the dining room and hugged again, hugged and looked into each others eyes, kissed, speechless, just overwhelmed from the moment. She was unable to say one word, all she felt was the need to feel him, to kiss him, to hold him and to be hold, while she felt the hunger in her body. He was looking so manly and great again. After a while they just followed their instinct. It was easy to know that they wanted the same. Smiling he started to undress her, while she opened his trouser and helped him out of his clothes. The bed was prepared but he turned her round, grasped her hips, bent her over the table and opened her legs, while diving into her wet hole, longing to feel her warmth and desire. She moaned. It was so good to feel him again and her hips started to describe little circles. He felt his needs and how he wished to let go, but he wanted to enjoy all of her and after some pleasant moves, he started to lick her butt hole until he felt, how ready she is and slowly entered his penis, while she helped him to glide inside. That felt so good. They both desired the same and while she started to move wild, showing him he can push and let go, he felt the need to come. With one hand he massaged her vagina and clit, while pushing harder into her butt, feeling her beginning ecstasy, while she breathed harder and moaned from pleasure, starting to loose control. Then she came and he could finally let go too, feeling her contractions and glided laughing outside her butt. He knew her too well, so grasped her again and started to massage her clit and vagina with his hands, ignoring her tries to escape, holding her down on that table while she cramped at the table, moaning harder again. He started to rub her G-spot in addition and suddenly she bowed with a moan and squirted all over his hands, nearly loosing her consciousness from that intense orgasm, but he hold her tight, feeling very content with himself but also happy for her, for both of them. She shivered and he knew that she always felt very dizzy, short after her intense orgasms, so he carefully lead her to the bed, covered her and hold her in his arms, until she relaxed and showed him that typical smile. The smile she always had after an orgasm. He loved to see that and he loved to see the love in her eyes. It was good to feel her nude body against his nude skin. It was good to be home again.

Chapter 19: Erotic Positions

„I have that new collection of positions on my handy" he told her on a nightly call „and I found some, which seem to be very inviting. I know already what I will do with you next time." She loved that. She loved to hear him making plans for joy, she loved when he described what he wanted to do with her. It made her shiver from lust. When she opened her mailbox the other morning, she found an email from him, where he added that erotic picture. It was a woman, laying on her back on a table, while the man was gliding inside her vagina, her legs on her shoulder. He had added some lines: "When I am there, I will lay you on that table we love so much and then I dive into both of your holes, while I lay your toy on your clit, driving you crazy." She felt the heat in her cheeks and thought about a good response. She found a book which described several positions but also some funny sexual games and decided to scan a very inviting picture for him. She mailed: "And here you see, how I will put oil between my breasts and butt and first massage your penis between my breasts, later rub him between my buttocks and then, I want to lick some honey from your shaft." The response came some hours later, when he was back from work. She found a picture, where a woman was blindfolded, but not bound. "Honey, I will blindfold your eyes and make you feel how I caress your skin with feathers, hair, soft toys, ice cubes and my tongue. I will take my time to give you sensual sensations, before I play with your clit and eat you out." She moaned from desire, when she read his words and went to bed, playing with her toys, when the phone rang. She knew it can only be him and spoke with a very rough voice, because she was already very aroused. "What are you doing?" he smiled. He knew and she knew that he knew. "Are you at work" she asked. "Yes". "Oh, just to let you know that I am nude now, I have a little anal plug in my butt, imagining you playing with me and I have my special toy in my hand. This second, I push one in my vagina, hmmm, and now the other at the clit." He breathed harder and tried to hide his arousal in front of his colleagues. She drove him crazy and he instantly wished to please her right now on his desk. He heard her moans and found his mouth getting dry and he knew from the kind of moans that she was short before coming. "Yes baby, do it, I love you" he whispered and then heard her come. He was hard and felt the pain, not being able to fulfill his needs this very second. She was a little devil, he knew how she enjoyed that right now, but he planned already some little revenges. "Wait until I get you between my fingers, honey, I make you squirt until you faint" he told her, what she answered with a rough and very pleased giggling. "Well, let deeds follow words" she answered with a huge grin. Next day she sent him a mail with a picture of a woman, who just started to lick a penis. "I can't wait to lick you like a candy." she added. When she opened her mails at night she found a picture of a woman with wide spread legs, but on her knees. A man licked her and she obviously was ecstatic. "I will eat you until you loose every feeling of day and night." Oh, how much she enjoyed that. They exchanged erotic pictures and so, the waiting time was shortened with sweet thoughts and very pleasant imaginations. They decided to examine erotic literature and videos to develop more possibilities for joy. It was so good to be on the same level.

Chapter 20: House of Sins

She was dreaming. It was evening in her dream, the daylight already fading, while she found herself deep in a forest, looking for the right way. She followed a small path which just opened in front her. She was not scared, she only felt nosy what to find in the forest. It was warm and soon she recognized that she wear no clothes. That seemed to be totally normal and she just wondered how she came as far being totally nude. The forest was not scary, in opposite. She felt like being a part of it, like being in her home, safe and protected. She also had time to enjoy the scent of the trees, of moss and humus, of the fir trees and the tree gum. With safe but also careful steps she went further, here and there diving under deep hanging branches. Suddenly the path ended in front of a clearing where she found a little wall with a gate. She opened the door and saw huge hedges, like a labyrinth, hiding a big wood house behind them. She passed fountains and statues of nude couples, she passed beautiful flower arrangements and was only accompanied by the murmur of a little stream, which seemed to flow nearby. She loved the murmur of water and found herself very comfortable, but also excited. Step for step, she made her way through those labyrinths and finally stood in front of the big house. "Hello?" she called, but nobody answered. She tried to find a door and went around the walls, but all she found was a sudden opening which seemed to be filled with bubbles or balloons. When she touched them, she was softly pushed inside the mass, feeling now the bubbles touching all of her body and skin. It was as if they know her secret places and she started to feel very aroused, trying to swim through this mass and somehow to escape from the arousal. But she was like swimming in a tenacious mass. It was hard to move on and somehow the arousal made it even harder to make steps, but finally she pushed herself out of a basin and climbed some steps higher. She found further basins, some filled with foam in rainbow colors and all with a wonderful erotic smell of red roses, musk, amber, vanilla and cinnamon. She sat down on a soft chair and decided to wait, what may happen, when the chair suddenly changed and moved and she felt something gliding directly into her pussy, filling her out and growing inside, while she tried to jump away. But she obviously was on a kind of vibrator chair because soon the massages started and she felt the reactions of her body. She tried to escape and finally managed to jump away, when she slipped and fall into one of those basins. She now was in the basin which smelled like musk with vanilla. She just wondered, how she know to differ all those scents, when she suddenly felt how her hands could not move from the side while something spread her legs and as if thousand tongues touched her legs and came higher to her labia and clit, diving deep into her holes and pleasing her until she screamed from lust. It did not stop, those invisible tongues made her come and have orgasm after orgasm until she suddenly woke up, feeling all the wetness between her legs and that she really had enjoyed an orgasm. Her body still shivering, she grasped the toy under her mattress and used the aroused body to come to a very quick orgasm, which was so intense that she could not move for a long while, before her heart beat seemed to normalize. She was still aroused from that strange dream but soon found back to a very deep sleep.

Chapter 20: Descent

While he had bought some red wine for their evening she had used the time to clean up the mess they had made together, especially those traces of lust, where he had made her squirt. He did not hear him coming back, because of the music. So he found her just on her knees, removing the water from her floor. When he entered the room and found her nude butt wiggling under her skirt, it was too inviting. He left the bottles right on the floor and jumped behind her, enjoying her surprised outcry and while holding her with one arm, he just opened his trouser and glided into her. She was laughing and tried to escape his grip, but now he had both hands free and enjoyed her wildness and how she loved those little challenges. Soon she followed his moves and started to move wild herself, just giving in to the joy. He felt already her contractions, when he saw the toy still laying on a chair and pressed it with high vibrations against her clit. That was too much for her and she tried to free herself again, but he knew how to hold it to make it pleasant. One hand added more gel and while he pushed now wilder into her holes he turned the vibrations on maximum, while holding her as strong as possible, because she was out of control now, moaning loud and moving with all her strength. Then she came, he felt it like force of nature, nearly pressing him out, but with that contractions and her arousing orgasm, he came and fall hard on her, holding her still tight but now also careful and tender. He kissed her and watched her face. She smiled, very pleased with his little "descent".

Chapter 21: Unexpected Joy

She had finished her daily routines and came back from the walk with her father's dog. So much had happened that year and some days had been nearly too much to bear. Day for day she watched her father's health getting worse, while her mother did not know how to cope with the situation, so she tried to hide her own pain as good as possible and to concentrate on making it easier for their family. Some days she found so dark and gray that it seemed to be nearly impossible to breath and on such days she had to force herself to do her duties, but she did them: step for step - and found relief in doing them. The only comfort was the knowledge how many bad times she had overcome in her past and she knew, deep there, behind that sometimes so very dark thoughts, she could count on a huge resource of strength. It was one of the days where she just focused on every single action. While creating a simple, but tasty meal, she enjoyed the scent of the herbs and the color of the ingredients. Cooking had always a very sensual, even erotic note for her and she decided to brighten her day a bit, burning on a beautiful candle with the flavor of vanilla. She brewed herself a tea and sat down, watching the autumn leaves of those beautiful trees in front of her kitchen window. Breath, she thought and she tried to relax and fall in one of those little in-between meditations, which helped her through her days.

Suddenly she froze on her chair. Somebody was outside her door. She waited, then heard something scratching, like a wrong key. Alerted she silently stood up and listened. Another wrong key. Her view touched the long kitchen knifes and she thought: well buddy, I am waiting when you think you can brake into my apartment. All her senses where highly alert now and she was ready to defend her home, when she heard a key turning round and open her entrance door. "Honey?"

That could not be possible! She jumped out of her hiding and hugged her mate, kissing him with a sound of joy. He was laughing. They had no time for explanations, but found themselves moments later in the middle of the cold floor, where she just had opened his trouser and started to ride on him, her butt direction to his face, so he could enjoy the wiggling buttocks, while she enjoyed his hands on her hips and how they just went crazy on each others body. After a while he draw her over his face and licked her until she came, while she tried to lick his penis. Suddenly she could not hold it any longer and moaned from the orgasm, which seemed to start from two points in her body. He was not ready yet and pushed her gently on her knees, taking her from behind, wild now until he could come, while she had her second orgasm, being so excited that her body just reacted on him. Ignoring the cold floor, they hugged each other and smiled happily.

"I got something to do in your near, baby. For one week, I can be with you night for night. Does this sound good?"

"Best music for my ears" she whispered happily. Time to share the simple food, which was tasty and she was happy that she had taken care so good of everything, that the apartment was nicely decorated and had a fresh and clean smell, that she had just washed and renewed her bed that morning, so she was able to give him a good 'welcome home'. But most of all, she was so happy about that unexpected joy to have him around. It made her days and nights so much easier and was the best contra-weight on this planet against all those sorrows.

Chapter 22: Storm is Over

It was a while until they had met, but she was used to those long weeks, even months of waiting for him. That year had taught her patience. She stood in front of the big mirror and touched her body, closing her eyes and thinking about her mate. She missed him so much and it was not always easy to have to overcome those long weeks before being able to meet again. But he had a job far away and was very busy, what she fully understood. She wanted to support him and not to make him feel bad nor add any pressure on his situation. He always told her about his tries to get a job closer to her and encouraged her to hold through, to go with him through that stormy time to enjoy the paradise in the end. Of course she was willing to wait for him. Love is a serious matter and fate something very special – and to find someone who seem to be on the same line on so many points is a rare gift. All she wanted was to build up a healthy partnership, to support each other, no manipulations, a lot of understanding for each other and to give each other some islands of joy and happiness in this difficult journey of life, of course also that free and pleasant sexual life. She got that too. She felt accepted the way she was and for that she was very grateful. But is was not always easy to cope with everything alone. She was used to it, but she missed his near at night and his company during the day. There is nothing wrong, I guess, to miss somebody I love, she thought and hugged herself dreamily. That is no weakness, that is what makes us human.

She decided to do herself something good and opened the well flavored body cream, dipping her fingers into the mass and starting to massage it all over her skin. Her nipples reacted at once and started to look nosy into the world, like little antennas of joy. She turned the heating higher and enjoyed the sensual moments, just concentrating on the feeling of the cold rich cream on her body. She loved the scent and it gave her the feeling of self-care and self-love, what was so important. So many people are longing for the love or respect of a person and never learned to love or respect themselves. But then, how can anybody expect somebody else to do this? When I never learn to value myself, I will always look for somebody who makes me happy. Of course a loved person causes happiness, but when I am not able to find happiness by myself, I start to draw energy from another person and start to burden him or her, what brings a relationship out of harmony and balance. Of course one can support each other in difficult times and times are normal too, where the balance is not working as well, but it is important to work on those matters, to solve them and find back to the own integrity.

She thought back to all those little rituals which had helped her through earlier difficult times and she smiled because she was able to do herself something good. She had bought a little decoration for her favorite room, she had bought a new flagrance and even if she had not the money for her favorite perfume, she had found a cheap one with a nice scent and enjoyed to use it for the day. She had also sorted out her own daily matters and changed what did not good or just wasted her time and blocked her from the creativity she needed for her ideas. All was on the way to heal and to improve and she was proud of herself and somehow content.

When she slipped into the soft silk of her Indian dress, she smiled and filled a little cup with water, then went back to her dining room and brought some white sheets and her artist colors. She remembered a time where she brought some drawings to an exposition, it was all so long ago, more than two decades. She once had possessed a good hand and was creating really nice drawings, being specialized on coal, sanguine and water colors. When did she stop painting? When she was twenty four? She remembered and let go the same moment. Totally different life, closed book of life. She remembered her first single time with twenty six and twenty seven, how she restarted to paint but found already that she had lost the safety in her lines. Later, when she had made little drawings with kids, she saw that she lost her good eye and ability to use those techniques, she had never learned but found out just by trying and reading books. Now, after some days of playing hermit and closing everything out as good as possible, she suddenly found her inspiration back, the longing to do some arts. She encouraged herself not to expect anything, any beautiful result, but just to let the colors flow. She opened her old box with the artist colors and hesitated, than choose one of the water color pencils and started to make some insecure lines. The room was warm and while she started to paint, her silk dress opened and glided from her shoulders down to her chair, but she totally ignored that, starting to find pleasure in those lines and to follow that kind of trance which she felt upcoming. Just do, she thought and chose the blue of her beloved river, she chose the green and the autumn leaves, she chose the brown and left white places for shine and glow, for reflections and while she continued she forgot her nude body and any feeling for time. She now dipped a paint brush softly into the water and started to blur over some lines, giving them that typical water color effect and those beautiful nuances. She even started to hum some melodies, totally forgetting the world around her.

That was how he found her. She had not heard him coming nor expected him. It was a surprise. He had silently opened her door, when he heard her singing. He smiled, she seemed to be content, that was good. Silently he came nearer and found her sitting with her back half towards the door, near the window to get enough daylight for her drawings. He had never seen her drawing before and stood there, hidden but enjoying to watch her. She was smiling and singing and seemed to be totally happy with her world. He watched the silk around her hips and her nude back, he watched her half discovered buttocks and found his body reacting. Anyway, the picture itself was so beautiful that he did not want to intrude. He enjoyed to watch her and silently placed his bag down the floor. She added colors and water and seemed to be in her element. Her hair was shining and he recognized that is was still long but some inches shorter than in his memory, but it looked great and healthy. Now in the daylight, there was a golden shimmer on it and it flow over her white shoulders. She dived the paint brush into the water and dived it now into another color, because she was not only working with water color pens any more. She watched the brush and while doing so, a blue drop landed on her breasts. He watched it running down her skin and discovered another water drop hanging on one of her nipples, shining in the sun like a little pearl. He wanted her so much. Suddenly she hesitated and seemed to breath in very deep, like a fox who gets the scent of some prey. She closed her eyes and slowly turned round to him.

She opened her eyes and found him smiling at her. "I suddenly felt you so intense, I suddenly was aware of your manly scent, I suddenly knew you are here." she whispered. He draw her gently from her chair, removed the remaining silk and lead her to the bed, just wanting to hold her a while but she saw his hunger and turned her back to him. Under her bed she always hided the gel and dropped it on her butt to allow him all his desires. But first he dived into her deep warm pussy, which was so wet and inviting. He kissed her back and neck, knowing how much she loved that, but she shortened the foreplay to let him fulfill his needs. While they moved, he heard her falling into that way of trance which helped her to let herself fall totally into pleasure and he knew her way of moaning and reacting. He loved her orgasms and he loved that she forgot the whole world around her, loving sex so much and following her instincts. He thought he cannot hold it much longer. When he felt her contractions and how she started to bow her back, he came and was nearly thrown out from her hole and in the same moment felt her muscles closing tight again. It was awesome, he loved it and slowly glided out of her body, holding her tight, while she shivered and still seemed to feel waves of lust. He carefully covered her and just gave her the comfort she needed. After a while he felt her eyes watching him. He saw tears but knew that they where tears of happiness, those treasured pearls of love. "Do you have some days work near again, love?" she asked him. "No, better, baby. I got that job we once talked about and so have only one hour to drive from work to be with you. Just two more weeks and then we have the weekends together and maybe even moments during the week." She was unable to speak and buried her head in his arms. He knew she was overwhelmed now from happiness and just gave her the embrace she needed. It was a long time before she was able to show her face but he saw the tears running down her cheeks and kissed them away. "It is all good, honey. All will be better now."

So the storm was over and the days of paradise began.

Chapter 23: Candlelight Dinner

It was Friday, when he returned from a long working day, happy to have those first weeks behind him. The new job was okay, the colleagues supportive and all seemed to glide over into a daily routine and regular rhythm. The way back home he wondered what she had prepared this time. He loved her cooking. Sometimes she took him on a little journey around the globe with her food, sometimes it was typical Bavarian cost and sometimes it was just a new creation, she had in her mind, but whatever she prepared, he really loved it and found her pleased about his content face. He opened the door and – as always – listened a short moment, allowing all his senses to get the situation. He heard her singing and then coming around to greet him with that happy glow of luck. A wonderful warm welcome and they enjoyed so much those moments they were able to share now, knowing too much about the difficult time which laid now behind them.

He was thinking to seduce her and saw the amused sparkle in her eyes, but then felt his hungry stomach and the scent of her cooking. She lead him to the dining room. Candles everywhere. She had prepared a beautiful table, decorated it with flowers and servicing, the new nice wine glasses and a nice table cloth. She kissed him and made him sit down, rubbing intentionally her butt against him. Promising. He smiled. Very soon she brought some plates with fresh figs and other fruits, she brought a fresh salad – one of her very own receipts. And she brought a wonderful prepared meet, which was so soft and tasty, that he thought to be a very happy man. He opened the bottles of new young red wine which was a specialty at this time of the year and filled their glasses. It was so delicious and they ate a while, silently enjoying. She smiled and looked very content, enjoying her own cooking as well. They toasted and refilled. "You made all beautiful and delicious honey, as always." he said while she smiled very happy and gave him a kiss. After the meal, they enjoyed some of the fruits and laid down to relax a bit, sharing their experiences of the day. As always he started to play with her nipples, while talking and opened her trousers to be able to feel her skin. "I want to feel you too" she whispered and so they both undressed, feeling still a bit too lazy to move. But they tenderly touched each others body and took their time to talk and caress, to hold, feel near and to enjoy the present moment. She kissed his forehead and lids, his nose and mouth, wandering gently upwards his throat, taking her time to place kisses on his skin and to circle around with her tongue. She made him turn round and warmed the massage oil between her hands, soon starting to massage his neck and back, carefully, tender and patient. He felt the need to glide away into a nap and tried to force himself not to follow it this time, he turned round and made her lay on her stomach to return the massage. "I will add some music" he said and started a collection of his favorite songs. It was amazing but they even shared the music taste. She purred from pleasure, enjoying his warm hands on her body. He recognized her softly moving hips and started to massage her legs, spreading them and touching her butt and her labia. Time to explore. She had closed her eyes and laid there, smiling and nosy. He made her lay down on her back again and gently blindfolded her eyes to hide the little surprise, he wanted to try out. He took the bottle with the new red wine and saw that it contained maybe a little rest for one glass. Perfect. She was already wet and ready for him, so he bent over her ears and told her "don't worry, baby, I will not cause you pain, relax" and she said "I know, love" then felt the cold bottle neck opening her labia and very slowly and carefully entering one or two inches of her hole. "I will not go deeper, don't worry" he said and she pressed his hands, touched about his care and knowing she can trust him to do her good. He carefully erected the bottle and made the new wine flow into her pussy. The cold prickle made her moan from surprise. He had placed a pillow under her hips to expose her vulva and filled all the remaining wine into her, while gently licking her clit, then started to remove the bottle carefully. "I will drink the wine from you now, honey" he said and she was highly aroused, unable to speak but just full of expectation. He started to press his mouth against her and began to please her with his tongue. It tasted like sin, the sweet wine and her sweet juices who seemed to built the perfect dessert after that meal. She moaned and moved her hips against him, trying to press his head closer. He hold her tight now, letting her no chance for her usual escaping games and started to dive his tongue deeper into her hole. She breathed harder and he moved her so that more wine was running out of her pussy, directly into his mouth. He went higher again and took his time to bring her clit between his lips, sucking it and wandering with his fingers around her holes. "Don't stop" she said and he knew how to continue and tried not to interrupt pressure and speed. Suddenly she reared up with a scream of lust and squirt directly on his breast. He wanted to come and took her legs high on his shoulder, just diving into her still contracting pussy and gave himself the relief he needed. He came and fall on her, holding her and they kissed. He was tired from work and thought to make a coffee to please more of her needs, but with a content grin, he recognized that once again she was sleeping before him, leaning against him with that very relaxed and cute impression on her face. He blew the candles out and went into spoon position, covering both of them. Only moments later, he found into deep and relaxed sleep himself.

Chapter 24: Crazy but Fun

They had to do some painting in their apartment and went to a local building center to get their tools. The whole way, she was teasing him, touching his penis while he drove his car, trying to concentrate on the traffic. He thought about just parking somewhere and pay her a revenge, but at such a warm and sunny day, people all seemed to spread out the floor like mushrooms. "Wait, when we are back, baby" he said, breathing deep, while she giggled content and very pleased. She loved that. She loved to provoke him to make him take her wild. They arrived and they went to buy some colors. "We need a ladder" she said. It would be good to have one at home, what do you think? "Try that one, he told her and placed a half-high ladder right behind the rack. She started to climb on it, when he pressed her against it, just opening her legs with his hand and giving her a quick intense massage on her clit. "Oh God, stop it!" she pleaded, nearly unable to stay silent, but he continued a short while before he stopped in time, helping her from the ladder. "You are mean" she protested and he was laughing content. "I am not ready with you" he answered, while she tried to look unimpressed but was obviously in a little uproar. As if nothing had happened, he innocently chose some paint brushes and things they may need, until they came to the cash point, having to wait in a long row. She looked at him with that very devilish impression, starting to press herself against his penis and rubbing carefully against him, trying not to get any attention from the surrounding people. Both of his arms where carrying tools, so he could not react nor do anything about that at the moment. She enjoyed it and started to massage him with one hand, completely pleased to find him getting hard. "It is too fair, my love" she grinned, being totally content with herself. Soon they had to pay and she followed him innocently whistling to their car. After putting all stuff into his car he opened her door for her, a courtesy, she always loved and appreciated so much. When she came to give him her "thank-you"-kiss, he just turned her and placed his jacket around them, hiding her from observant eyes, than opened his trouser, brought her skirt high and entered her pussy. She giggled but had no chance to escape. Cars passed and people came near, so he stopped the little game but found her cheeks red from desire and expectation. When he drove, she started to rub him again, enjoying that now it was he, who was on her mercy. But this time, he chose another way and against his usual habit, drove the car faster. She giggled again and started a provoking play with her breasts with one hand, knowing that he will get it. The other hand continued to open his trouser and play with him. He found a little path into the forest and made a hard curve, just to park and jump out of the car. She squealed and jumped out herself, giggling and laughing and started to run away, but no chance. He got her and took her deep into the thicket. There he just took her without caring anymore for anybody to hear her moans. He pushed her hard and rubbed her clit until she squirted again and they came together. She nearly fall on her knees, but he was holding her and made her relax in his arms. "You are a very bad girl" he whispered and she was grinning from one ear to the other.

Chapter 25: Parachuting

It was the day where an old dream of her fulfilled: to parachute down with her love, being connected as a tandem. She barely found sleep the night before, while he seemed to be totally himself, calm and obviously unimpressed. He watched her being nervous and excited, but smiled because she behaved like a kid, waiting for St. Claus. It was a long way to drive but finally they arrived. They where not alone, some sky divers went to the plain for training. But first he helped her into a neat dress and into a leather helmet. He gave her some glasses and helped her climb into the gear, fixing it around her legs, hips and shoulder. She was laughing about the strange outfit and even more, when she tried to walk halfway normal, what seemed to be impossible. He watched her and found no signs of fear, just joy and excitement. He showed her how to stand before the jump, how to go into her knees and place her hands around the girth at the shoulder and also explained her, how she has to sit down on him in the plain, to let him connect with her. "Before we jump, you lean your head backwards against my shoulder, honey, ok?" She nodded, too excited to speak. He explained her more, how to react on his signs, when he touches her shoulder, how to place her hands and what will happen until the landing. She felt so comfortable with his calm voice, safe and protected. Finally the plain started. She did not know if it was as hot or if she just sweated from excitement, but it was not too much place and all seemed to be a bit uncomfortable. The more pleasant was the beautiful view outside. She loved to fly. He watched her but developed only joy, no fear. He grinned. Faster than expected, they reached the high of 4000 meters. First the sky divers left, what always seemed to catapult the plain higher, but then it was their turn. The world outside seemed to be far away and like a miniature game, unreal and beautiful the same time, but she had not too much time to think, just went slight into her knees and placed her head backwards against his shoulder, as he had learned her before. Before she could imagine, they already jumped and in those sixty seconds of free falling, she was simply too overwhelmed with all those in-flooding impressions. It was as if things happened faster than her mind could follow, but very soon she felt his touches on her shoulder and had to change her hand position, while he opened the parachute. The sudden strong tag surprised her, even he had explained her before, that it will happen that way. But then they suddenly where gliding.

It was so amazing, she found herself laughing loud and giggling, being nearly ecstatic from joy. Such a liberty, such a beauty, how beautiful that planet was, how great the flight. She felt like a bird and wished she could stay in the air forever, just feeling his near and comfort. He was happy to feel her joy and they both enjoyed to share this experience. For him it was not new but it was something else, to do this because of a job or with a beloved woman. It was just awesome. Meanwhile with his help, she had changed herself into a sitting position and he let her use the control cables. They made wild curves, left and right and a roller coast ride was nothing in comparison. They both laughed and enjoyed the moment. After nearly eight minutes they arrived and managed a proper landing. He helped her to disconnect but she jumped back, embracing and kissing him, while gleaming from joy and happiness. They kissed and wanted to forget the whole world, but had to carry the equipment first. As soon as possible they went into a private chamber, longing to celebrate that experience. They only half undressed, he sat down on a chair, while she sat down on him, still longing to be as close to him as possible. Than they started to move and soon where carried away from their needs. When they both came, she moaned and thought, she will loose her mind. It was so intense. She just wished she could jump again and again and fly forever. He smiled at her. "You was not scared one single moment, right?" "No" she grinned. He laughed and was proud about his girl. What a wild one!

Chapter 26: Body Massage

One of those days, where the humid cold wind seemed to blow through all the bones. Since the morning, the landscape was buried under a thick foggy cover. People seemed to hide behind her jackets and ducked their heads behind collars and shawls.

She stood behind the kitchen window, preparing some hot tea and watched, how the last remaining leaves where torn from their branches. He had called few minutes before, to let her know he is on his way. He sounded tired. She turned the lamb in the oven and prepared the table, then, with a smile, placed the massage oil close to the heating, to carefully warm it up. She wanted to make him a wonderful, relaxed evening, where he may forget the hard week and the cold, stormy weather. She went to the bedroom, closed the window and turned the heating on. It should be warm and comfortable. The apartment had already the very inviting smell of the good food, she prepared the glasses and the wine. All was ready, just the meat needed one more hour, just the time he had to drive due to that weather conditions. She used the time to take a shower. It was so good to feel the warm water running down the skin and she took her time to massage her body with foam and water. For a short moment she thought to please herself, but she wanted to be ready with everything in time, so dried herself with the rough towel until her skin was pink. Time for her body cream and time to enjoy the flagrance while caressing the soft emulsion into her skin. She started with her hands and arms, the shoulders and the breasts, always playing there a little bit longer, then her belly and but, her back, the feet until the knees and upper legs, until she was all shrouded into the wonderful scent. She closed her eyes and enjoyed the moment, then – with a view to the watch – chose the fresh clothes and made herself ready. Hair, lipstick and finished, she was content and smiled. Back to the kitchen she finished the sauce for the lamb and started to place the side dishes on warmed plates, trying to give all a nice and inviting arrangement. The scent was fine and she felt hungry herself.

Soon afterward, she heard his steps coming up the stairs. He took them slowly and she heard his tiredness.

When she opened the door, they just hugged for a while. She left him in peace but they both smiled and it was good to be together. "Hmm, it smells good" he said and she led him to the seat. "Sit down, my love, I bring the food." He gave her a kiss and followed her to the kitchen to help carrying the plates. He knew, her day has been long too and he always tried to give her a hand, what made her smile. Alone that smile was worth the effort. She burned the candle on and one descent light in a corner. "Is it too dark?" "No, perfect, sit down to me." They ate and enjoyed the meal. "Baby, are you mad when I lay down a while?" "Of course not, come with me, but get off your clothes, I will make you a massage." He smiled and both undressed. "Lay on your stomach, love" she said and took the warmed massage oil bottle. Nude as she was, she climbed on his nude butt. She started to drop the oil on his skin, enough to disperse it all over his back. Then she started to massage his neck. With little circles and soft pressing touches and movements, she wandered from inch to inch of his body, slowly massaging every part, while she enjoyed his beautiful strong shoulders and the shine of his skin. She loved to watch him, she always thought to paint him. Her fingers wandered to his shoulders and arms, back to the neck and deeper down the back, she took her time with the backbones and went deeper down to the buttocks, then started to massage in waves from the spine to the sides, upwards again, than the spin downwards. He grunted content and felt the sweet heaviness in his body. When she finished his back, she covered the part and went down to his legs. It was a wonderful feeling to massage him and she loved to cause him comfort. They still had not talked about their days but it was obvious that he just wanted to relax now. The weekend just started and they had enough time for talking. It was totally okay. She wandered down his feet and made him gently turn round. Then she started a reflexology and took her time with it. When she finished the second foot, she heard him snore and smiled. She covered him good, turned the heating down and went back to the kitchen to clean up and enjoy the hot tea from the thermos flask. She went to her massage chair and enjoyed a little nap on it, while feeling the massage waves and the heating of the seat. About two hours had passed, when she heard him using the bathroom. She just enjoyed another cup of hot tea, when he came to give her a long hug. "That was so good, baby, thank you." "Most welcome, I am happy to do you good." "And now, it is your turn, come with me." He had already warmed the room and lead her to the bed. He undressed her and made her lay down on her stomach. Now it was him who massaged her with the oil. She loved a back massage and started to purr like a cat. When he went down to her butt, he could not resist to follow the line deeper between her legs. She wiggled her butt and grinned. With two hands he started to massage her buttocks and then slipped down to her labia. The oil made her skin shine and it aroused him to see her that way, already waiting for more. He dived his finger into her pussy and yes, felt already her wet juices. She opened her legs and than suddenly he felt such a hunger, he parted her legs even wider and glided into her warm hole. She moaned and pressed her hips against him. Then they changed the positions, so that she was laying sidewards before him. They managed without losing connection and soon started to move careful. It was a very tender position. Even if he was unable to get very deep into her, he enjoyed being able to massage her clit and to watch her butt, while she enjoyed the comfort and feeling of care and protection. They had time and played very slowly. After a while she turned round and sat down on him. She still did not want to move faster, just playing and enjoying the different feelings. He was teasing her a bit and saw her body's reactions, but still did not allow her to come. She had closed her eyes now, her head laying backwards in her neck. She described little circles with her hips, pleasing herself with his penis in a rhythm of her own, but still very slowly. Then he felt his needs getting stronger and made her lay down on her knees, while gliding again into her vagina. She was all wet now and he loved the feeling. When he started to move, he heard the sound of her clasping buttocks against him and it turned him on. She moved wilder now and he started to please her clit with one hand, while taking her faster now. She grasped the bed, the cover, the pillow, starting to loose control and just reacting, just giving in to the feeling and letting herself fall into it. Then she came, he felt her contractions and her moan, while she bowed her back and so he let go too and came. He turned her round and licked her juices. She was swollen from lust and he licked her so intense that she had another orgasm few minutes later. It smelled like honey and herbs, sweet and spicy and he licked her dry, while she breathed happy and fulfilled. "That was the medicine I needed" she whispered, while kissing him long and intense.

Epilog

Thus ended the material I chose for my book. There where some other hints and short entries, but most of them changed towards plans and dreams, how to spend the time together. I wanted to focus on the erotic short stories and hope very much that I did those two justice with my interpretations.

I made one change, in spite of that conversation on our last walk together: After using the lover's names in the beginning, I had decided to write only the neutral "he" and "she" in my stories, to give the reader the possibility to identify and use the fantasies for the own pleasure and imaginations. I hoped that would be okay for those two, and got the response a few days later:

Dear Hilde,

hope you do fine. First of all we both want to thank you so much for bringing our sweetest memories back to us. We now use your book as little erotic lecture and William loves to read those stories to me, while I lean against his nude body, drinking a glass of red wine. It is always an inspiration and it really turns us on to find ourselves acting in a book. Somehow we felt as if you have secretly watched us, so close did you come to the real scenes.

Concerning the names: Don't worry, our vanity is fulfilled in being mentioned in your foreword.

I often think back to our walks together along that beautiful river.

Hope your inspiration will lead you to many more books. We even started another diary and who knows, maybe in future you love to continue your project.

Once again: Thank you, take care and feel a big embrace

Yours,
Hanna

Acknowledgment

I want to thank Hanna and William for their frank attitude, their trust and the will to share their very intimate stories with me and my readers.

I also want to thank my love for his encouragement and for loving me like I am.

And last but not least I want to thank you for choosing and reading my book. I hope you had a pleasant time with it.

Further books of the authoress

Gedanken zur Selbstfindung, 2nd edition, 2010
ISBN-13: 978-3837054842
9,90 €
Language: German-English*

Mosaik des Lebens, 2nd edition, 2010
ISBN-13: 978-3837044720
9,90 €
Language: German

Gesammelte Gedichte, 2nd edition 2010
ISBN-13: 978-3839141083
11,80 €
Language: German-English*

Zukunftsdeuten mit Skatkarten, 1st edition 2008
ISBN-13: 978-3837067989
9,90 €
Language: German

*Only some of the included poems are in English, while most parts of the books are written in German.